"A no-frills, no-nonsense guide to 78 ski tours in the Cascades. If getting into and out of the wilderness safely is your goal, this is your book."

— *Neil Stebbins*
POWDER Magazine

"An extremely useful guide for intermediate to advanced skiers seeking the backcountry experience in Washington state. Gives a broad perspective of specific backcountry ski tours along with a heavy emphasis on safety and preparation."

— *NORDIC WEST Magazine*

"Rainer Burgdorfer and The Mountaineers have reason to be proud of this ambitious and carefully crafted effort. Tour descriptions are not so abbreviated as to be unusable to the exploring skiers. More important, an effort has been made here to teach why the backcountry Cascades of winter must be approached with an eye and ear to the weather and the conditions it breeds."

— *Gordy Holt, SEATTLE*
POST-INTELLIGENCER

"An intelligent guide to the burgeoning sport of backcountry skiing in Washington, which, besides having complete, easily followed information on a large collection of trails, also contains an appropriate regard for low-impact skiing — something that is absolutely necessary if we're to continue such skiing. Author Burgdorfer is to be commended."

— *Ginny Hostetter, Senior*
Editor,
CROSS COUNTRY SKIER

Cascade high routes are unique in the U.S.; Clark Mountain — Tour 44 (Photo: Joe Cattellani).

BACKCOUNTRY
SKIING
IN WASHINGTON'S CASCADES

RAINER BURGDORFER

The Mountaineers, Seattle

The Mountaineers: Organized 1906
". . . to explore, study, preserve and enjoy
the natural beauty of the Northwest."

Copyright © 1986 by The Mountaineers

Published by The Mountaineers
306 Second Avenue West, Seattle, Washington 98119

Published simultaneously in Canada by
Douglas & McIntyre Ltd.
1615 Venables Street
Vancouver, British Columbia V5L 2H1

Manufactured in the United States of America
Edited by Barbara Chasen
Maps by Rainer Burgdorfer
Cover design by Elizabeth Watson
Layout by Bridget Culligan
Cover photos by Gary Brill

Library of Congress Cataloging in Publication Data
Burgdorfer, Rainer, 1948-
    Backcountry skiing in Washington's Cascades.

    Bibliography: p.
    Includes index.
    1. Cross-country skiing — Washington (State) — Guide-
books.   2. Cross-country skiing — Cascade Range — Guide-
books.   3. Cascade Range — Description and travel — Guide-
books.   4. Washington (State) — Description and travel —
1981-   — Guide-books.   I. Title.
GV854.5.W33B87   1986   796.93'09797   86-18133
ISBN 0-89886-129-2

0   9   8   7   6
5   4   3   2   1

Contents

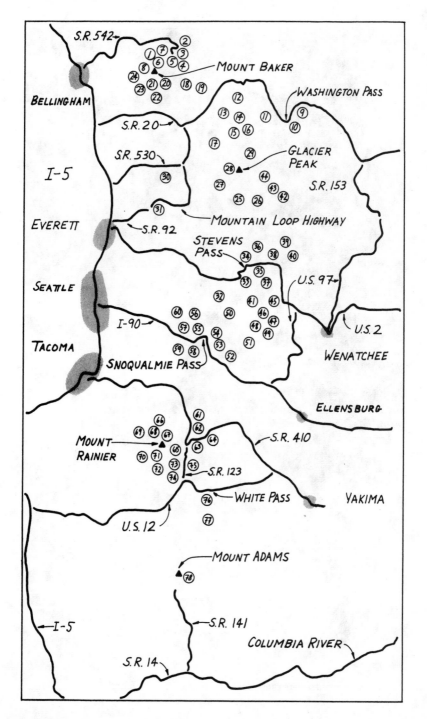

Note the ice axe and self-arrest grips. Silver Star Glacier — Tour 9 (Photo: Gary Brill).

Preface

This guide was written for two main reasons: first, to get you to great backcountry skiing in the Washington Cascades; second, to help you come back alive and happy.

Northwest Ski Trails, written by Ted Mueller and published by Mountaineers Books in 1968, was the first comprehensive description of Washington snow tours written for alpine skiers. It became outdated and has been out of print since 1975.

Other guides, such as the comprehensive *Snow Trails* by Gene Prater and *Cross-Country Ski Trails of Washington's Cascades and Olympics* by Tom Kirkendall and Vicky Spring, emphasize the needs of snowshoe travelers and novice and intermediate touring skiers. These tours tend to take place on gentler terrain than the trips described in *Backcountry Skiing in Washington's Cascades*. Some of the tours described in this guide have names and destinations similar to tours described in *Cross-Country Ski Trails of Washington's Cascades and Olympics*, but the tours are substantially different because of alternative, steeper descent routes. *Backcountry Skiing in Washington's Cascades* describes tours suitable for both Nordic and alpine ski mountaineers who long for great downhill runs, excellent views, and an alpine experience.

People are flocking to the Cascade Mountains in unprecedented numbers, in every season, using all manner of conveyances. Fortunately, either by virtue of its gradient or its inclusion in wilderness or national park areas, the terrain of greatest interest to backcountry skiers is frequently off-limits to machines.

Nevertheless, the issue of multiple use (in this case, different types of recreational use) must be addressed by those who want to continue enjoying safe and relatively quiet snow tours. Vilifying outdoor users who do not share the human-power ethic accomplishes little but polarization. It is up to skiers and snowshoers to engage in an intelligent lobbying effort to secure safe, quiet approaches and touring terrain. Write to your representatives! Protect your interests!

Affiliation with a conservation-oriented outdoor group is strongly suggested. Regional outdoor clubs are given here.

The Mountaineers, 300 3rd Avenue West, Seattle, WA 98119
(also branches in Tacoma, Everett, and Olympia)
The Mazamas, 909 N.W. 19th Street, Portland, OR 97232
Spokane Mountaineers, P.O. Box 1013, Spokane, WA 99210

Skagit Valley Alpine Club, P.O. Box 513, Mount Vernon, WA 98273

Sierra Club, 1516 Melrose Way, Seattle, WA 98104

Written comments to U.S. Forest Service officials urging equitable allocation of trails and roads to foot-powered travelers can get results. U.S. Forest Service and National Park headquarters follow.

U.S. Forest Service, Pacific Northwest Regional Headquarters, 319 S.W. Pine Street, Portland, OR 97208

Gifford Pinchot National Forest, 500 W. 12th Street, Vancouver, WA 98660

Mount Baker–Snoqualmie National Forest, 1022 1st Avenue, Seattle, WA 98104

Wenatchee National Forest, 3 S. Wenatchee Avenue, Wenatchee, WA 98801

Okanogan National Forest, 219 2nd Avenue South, Okanogan, WA 98840

Mount Rainier National Park, Tahoma Woods, Star Route, Ashford, WA 98304

North Cascades National Park, Ross Lake and Lake Chelan National Recreation Areas, Sedro Wooley, WA 98284

It is essential that backcountry skiers make their voices heard to secure adequate resources for their recreational needs and for the needs of future generations.

This project could not have been completed without the good will and support of friends, co-workers, and other interested persons: Harry Hendon, Donal O'Sullivan, Bob Odom, Barb Sherrill, Keith, Ken, and Kerry Ritland and Suze Woolf were enthusiastic supporters of this venture.

Ann Cleeland, Steve Whitney, and Donna DeShazo from The Mountaineers Books, and Barbara Chasan, the editor, made final assembly of the book a joy. Lynn McMurdie assisted in compiling the sections on Cascade weather, and Ken White of the U.S. Forest Service offered useful criticisms and information.

Joe Firey and Steve Barnett helped to check tour descriptions and provided needed perspective on techniques and equipment. Linda Givler's insightful comments helped insure the accuracy of this guide.

Special acknowledgment is due to Gary Brill, professional skiing and mountaineering guide and friend. His excellent photographs and constructive criticism enhanced the utility and appearance of the guide, and his experience and safety-conscious attitude helped me come to terms with risk in recreational activities.

Finally, I'd like to thank all those people, too numerous to mention, who have had a hand in teaching me what skiing is all about.

Rainer Burgdorfer
Seattle, 1986

Introduction

Why would anybody hike five miles to ski the equivalent of five chair-served runs? Imagine untracked snow, mind-blowing views, and pride in feeling your body meet a physical challenge, and you have one answer. Use this guide and find 78 more reasons.

A decade ago, Cascade ski touring was the province of hard-core ski mountaineers. Increasing levels of physical fitness, modern lightweight equipment, and greater knowledge of mountain safety have made backcountry skiing feasible for the "rest of us." Both alpine and Nordic touring equipment now offer the degree of control and safety necessary to make backcountry skiing practical and fun for most people.

You do need more than equipment to ski the backcountry safely. You also need skill, local knowledge, judgment, and a safety-conscious attitude. This guide provides some of the necessary local knowledge. You must provide the skill, judgment, and attitude.

Time your tour to return before dusk (Photo: Ken Ritland).

HOW TO USE THIS GUIDE

Selecting a ski tour is easy with this guide: Use the Seasonal Cross Reference table on page 224 to pick a tour based on the season, or pick a tour in a specific area by turning to the table of contents.

Each tour description consists of a summary, a map, and a written description. Each summary gives the starting location and elevation, the tour's high point, the best time to make the trip, the tour length, the level of difficulty, and the necessary maps. The summary, which also includes the level of avalanche potential, should help you match a tour to your circumstances.

The start point is where you leave your car. This location may vary, depending on road conditions or snow levels. The high point is the elevation of a feasible objective of the tour. Elevations, where given, are approximate.

The best time suggests a good season for the tour. Weather and snow conditions will vary from year to year, so this suggestion must be taken with a view to recent weather patterns.

Tour length indicates whether or not a tour is an overnight trip, its

Ski in control, keeping well away from terrain hazards (Photo: Gary Brill).

approximate round-trip length in miles, and how many hours of round-trip travel may be expected for a reasonable party, using modern equipment, in good conditions. You can expect to take longer if you are using 1970s skis and boots, encounter poor snow conditions, or are carrying overnight gear on a day trip. If conditions are ideal, you may beat the estimate by half. While some of the stated time estimates for specific tours might seem short to those who have hiked the same routes in summer months, remember that ski descents can be significantly faster than hiking descents.

Level of difficulty indicates overall and special requirements of the tour, including the level of avalanche potential. *None of the tours described in this book is for novice skiers. Every tour requires at least intermediate skiing skills.* The tours are rated intermediate or advanced, depending on a combination of the difficulty of skiing and other factors likely to be encountered. "Navigation" indicates that map, compass, possibly an altimeter, and close attention to route-finding are essential for reaching the tour objective in a reasonable amount of time. Attempting a tour outside of the suggested season may affect the difficulty rating. It should be noted that snow conditions have as much, or more, to do with difficulty as any factors intrinsic to the tour.

Intermediate tours require the ability to ski up and down moderate slopes, turning at will. An intermediate tour will require some experience with winter camping and survival, and with mountaineering. Such a tour will also require familiarity with the basics of avalanche hazard avoidance. Most tours will require some navigation, especially when snow obscures trails.

An advanced tour requires a high degree of skill in all aspects of ski mountaineering, including avalanche hazard avoidance. When corniced ridges and other obstacles make travel difficult, it is so noted. Tours calling for extreme skiing (if you fall, you die) are not considered here.

Current versions of USGS and Green Trails* maps are listed for reference. Where possible, USGS 7.5-minute maps are recommended for ease of navigation. Otherwise, Green Trails maps are recommended because they generally contain more recent information than USGS maps and because they show important and useful travelers' information on their reverse sides. The route sketches are intended to be used in addition to, not as a substitute for, Green Trails or USGS maps.

Approach roads are identified by the new Forest Service numbers, and mileages to key locations are rounded to the nearest tenth of a

---

*Wherever "Green Trails" is used in this book it refers to the registered trademark of Green Trails, Inc.

mile. If you are using an older mountaineering guide for historical information about a route, the USFS "Cross-Over List" (U.S. Government Printing Office Document #993-146) can help you convert old road numbers to new and vice versa.

Where there is more than one approach, the primary approach is described, with advantages and drawbacks discussed in the text. Directions are given using points of the compass. Landmarks and elevations are given when helpful for routefinding.

ETIQUETTE

Customs change. Ever-increasing numbers of outdoor enthusiasts place heavy pressure on the alpine and subalpine environment. Backcountry skiers must do their part to reduce the adverse impact of their passage.

- Defecate away from streams, lakes and low areas. The highly motivated ecophile may even "pack it out."
- Carry litter out.
- Leave your dog at home. There are very real alpine hazards for pets: moats, cliffs, tree wells, avalanches, hypothermia, and porcupines. In addition, dogs are less fastidious about toilet habits than sophisticated backcountry skiers.
- Step out of the way of snowmobiles or faster skiers, especially when skiing a defile. Etiquette demands that speedy skiers and snowmobilers avoid persons moving more slowly; prudence suggests you protect yourself.
- Do not cut conifer boughs for shelter or sleeping platforms.
- Do not block other vehicles parked at roadheads. Be certain your car is parked completely off the public highway. This means on the shoulder side of the white edge-line.
- Buy a Sno-Park permit and display it properly. (It's the law.) Your participation in this program provides powerful justification for allocating trails and forests to human-powered recreationists.
- Respect property rights. Rather than sneak in, write to the Forest Service, the National Park Service, or Washington State Parks Sno-Park Committee to voice your opinion on the need for reasonable parking areas.

SAFETY CONSIDERATIONS

The tours described in this guide are not necessarily safe for you or your party. Every tour, and backcountry skiing in general, entails

Preparing for the descent from Camp Muir — Tour 73 (Photo: Gary Brill).

unavoidable risks from terrain, weather, and avalanches. (Also see "Avoiding Avalanches" on page 26.) Every skier who uses this guide and ventures onto these slopes assumes and must accept these risks, as well as responsibility for his or her own safety. Remember that local route conditions may change rapidly, sometimes in a matter of hours. Routes safe in mid-morning may be dangerous hours later due to weather or snow changes. You can minimize risks by developing a base of experience, being prepared, and fostering a safe attitude. The Recommended Reading List in the back of this book should be considered "must read" material.

An essential part of preparedness is an awareness of your own resources, including equipment, skiing or climbing skills, and physical stamina *on the day of the tour.* Many of the springtime tours, for example, take place above timberline and involve ascending or descending steep, exposed slopes. Wind, time of day, or cloud cover may make these slopes soft or very icy. For tours involving such terrain, knowing how to use and carrying an ice ax and crampons may be essential to your safety. If the conditions are dangerous, choose a different tour. It is simply not worth getting hurt.

Backcountry skiers must rely on self-rescue, including first aid and evacuation, in the event of accident. The right equipment (see

Slab avalanches sometimes involve large amounts of snow (Photo: Joe Cattellani).

Appendix A) is essential. Knowledge and attitude are also important.

A reasonable level of physical fitness helps backcountry skiers enjoy their tours and provides an extra margin of safety. A tired skier falls more often and increases the likelihood of injuries to himself. A sprained ankle or knee is no joke two miles from the car on a winter evening.

Skiers should ski within their ability, with an eye to the consequences of a fall. "I can't ski that steep bit there; a fall would put me into that moat or over that cliff band." You can always take your skis off and climb down if necessary.

Backcountry skiers should consider the following special equipment an essential part of their kit: compatible avalanche transceivers (one per person); nonbreakable shovels (one per person); and avalanche probes. Avalanche victims who have been buried less than six feet deep and were in parties equipped with transceivers have experienced over a 95 percent live recovery rate (see Tony Daffern's *Avalanche Safety for Skiers and Climbers*). This remarkable outcome is a powerful argument for carrying the added equipment and knowing how to use it well. Practice using your transceiver!

This guidebook is based on personal experience and should be used as an aid rather than a substitute for your own judgment. You are truly on your own.

These warnings are not intended to keep you out of the backcountry. Thousands of people take safe and enjoyable ski tours every year. However, one aspect of the beauty, freedom, and excitement of the backcountry is the presence of risks normally hidden by the veil of civilization. When you ski the backcountry, you assume those risks. To meet the challenge, you must exercise your own independent judgment and common sense.

KEY TO TOUR MAPS

Approach Roads: Main   **— — — —**
               Secondary   **— — — —**

Main Route   **━━━━━━━━━**

Alternative   **· · · · · · · · · · · · · · · · ·**
    or
Optional Routes

Areas of Special Concern

Early-season skiing near Liberty Bell — Tour 10 (Photo: Ken Ritland).

Part I | Learning to Love Cascade Snow

CASCADE WEATHER AND SNOW

If you don't learn weather basics in Washington, you'll spend more time skiing crud or ice than powder or corn snow. Worse, you may give up skiing because "it's terrible in Washington." You don't have to become a weather expert. An amateur meteorologist doesn't require mathematics but does need to ask the right kinds of questions. Then he'll know which tours are best under a given set of conditions. For example, where is the best place to ski during inversion periods? How can convergence zones help in the search for fine skiing? Where is there good skiing if it hasn't snowed for weeks or months?

Air masses are the basic building blocks of regional weather. An air mass is a large (say half a continent) body of air that has taken on some of the characteristics of the surface below it. Since the ocean warms and cools slowly, marine air masses tend to be mild and moist. Continental (over land) air masses tend to have greater extremes (and more rapid changes) of temperature and are generally drier than marine air masses.

During the winter in Washington, there are generally westerly winds at all levels of the atmosphere. Most of the surface air is therefore of marine origin, except where it's blocked by the Cascade Mountains. The Cascades present an effective barrier to surface flows. This blockage allows continental air masses to predominate east of the crest and is the main reason for the drier, cooler (in winter) eastside climate.

Winter brings frequent "storms" to the Pacific Northwest. (Storms are more correctly called midlatitude cyclones, but the colloquial expression is used in this guide.) Storms generally bring clouds and rain to lower regions and snow to the mountains. Sometimes these systems penetrate to inland areas, resulting in a modified marine climate in eastern Washington. Storms consist of a low pressure center (a "low"), a "cold" front, and sometimes a "warm" front and an "occluded" front. A low pressure center is the part of the system where the air pressure is lowest. A front is the narrow transition zone between two different air masses. Fronts are marked by clouds, precipitation, changes in wind direction and speed, and a sudden drop in air temperature and pressure (pressure trough). A warm front replaces existing cooler air with advancing warmer air from the south; a cold front brings cooler air from the north. Often, warmer air precedes cold fronts and colder air. In this case, the warmer air produces higher freezing levels and rain in the mountains while along and behind the cold front there are lower freezing levels and snow.

There are occasions when western Washington experiences continental weather. This occurs when the boundary between the arctic continental air mass in Canada and the marine air mass over the Gulf of Alaska passes through western Washington. A typical scenario involves a snow storm followed by a period of clear skies and low temperatures. Skiing can be excellent during these periods if the northerly winds associated with them are not too strong.

Systems are imbedded in upper-level air currents called the jet stream. The jet stream "carries" systems along its path toward the west coast of North America. If the jet stream comes from the northwest, any system imbedded in this flow will generally be cool. If such a system also contains lots of moisture, it will be a good snow producer. When the jet stream comes from the southwest, systems associated with it will tend to be warm and result in high freezing levels, rain instead of snow in the mountains, and extreme avalanche danger. If the jet stream flows "around" the Washington area (the weather forecaster calls this "a ridge over Washington"), systems will be diverted to the north or south. When this occurs in midwinter, lower-level air will stagnate and cool, while the mountains will experience sunshine and gradually warmer temperatures (and thickening crusts). This situation is called an inversion, in which lower-level air is colder than upper-level air.

Two local factors that help enhance snowfall in the Washington Cascades are orographic lifting and convergence zones.

Orographic (caused by mountains) lifting occurs when an air mass moving east (or west) is forced upward over the Cascade (or any mountain) range and expands. As the air expands, it cools. This cooling causes water vapor to condense and fall out as precipitation on the windward side of the range. The average temperature drop is

3.5 degrees Fahrenheit per thousand feet of elevation. On the average, if it is 45 degrees (F) in Seattle, it is about 32 degrees near 3000 feet in the Cascades. As the air mass crosses the Cascades, it descends and warms, becoming drier in the process. That's why the climate is drier on the east side of the Cascades.

Convergence zones occur when the coastal airflow is moving west–northwest and maintains relatively constant speed and direction. The moving air is split by the Olympics and converges on the lee side over Puget Sound and the west slope of the Cascades. When the air converges, it is forced to rise and consequently cool. The result is greater than "normal" precipitation locally, usually in the north Puget Sound region. Sometimes this enhancement extends to the western slopes of the Cascades, causing locally heavy snowfall near Stevens or Snoqualmie Pass.

FINDING GOOD SKIING

Although skiing is properly a "snow sport" rather than a seasonal sport, the Cascade season can be conveniently thought of as beginning in October or November and ending in July. Good early-season skiing is provided by cool storms, which sometimes dump a few feet of snow at higher elevations.

Watch the weather reports on television, especially the satellite photo and the synopsis: If the jet stream is coming from the northwest and has a marine path, it will likely be cool and dump dry snow at higher elevations. Good skiing can then be found on heather benches and permanent snowfields. You must be prepared to hike a bit but will be able to regale your friends with tales of November powder. Beware of windslab formation (see the avalanche discussion) resulting from high winds; choose tours that are not exposed to windslab danger or take alternative approaches and descents to avoid hazardous areas.

If the jet stream is bringing storms from the southern Pacific, they will tend to be warm and wet, often raising the snow level above timberline. Under these circumstances, touring is not recommended. Even with snow levels at moderate elevations, heavy, wet snowfall will result in poor and dangerous touring conditions. Skiing above timberline during storms is not recommended.

Even during periods of little snowfall there is often good skiing, so long as there is enough snow to cover rocks and stumps (wear kneepads). Snow on north-facing or tree-sheltered slopes often maintains a soft surface due to radiative cooling and surface hoar formation. When inversions blanket mountain valleys, you can ski shady places and find hoar or dry snow on north-facing slopes.

Don't count on easy skiing on south-facing slopes during inversions since there is usually not enough sun in midwinter to melt a frozen crust.

Early-season ski tours often require a hiking approach (Photo: Ken Ritland).

Our marine climate sometimes results in winter freezing levels above 4000 feet. Skiing tends to be poor under these conditions, with an important exception: the presence of easterly winds at the passes. Winds from the east reduce air temperatures there so that snow conditions may be much better than overall freezing levels would suggest. This occurs when a high-pressure area lies east of Washington and a lower pressure lies to the west. Watch for this on the evening weather report.

As the season progresses, the days get longer. Slopes that get loaded by March and April storms can receive relatively large amounts of sunshine. The result is often rapidly increasing avalanche danger and deteriorating skiing conditions, particularly on south slopes. During winter and spring a good rule of thumb is to expect unstable conditions any time temperatures exceed those of the recent past. For example, if average daytime temperatures in Seattle have been 60 degrees (F) and they are now 70 degrees, you should expect instability. A change in average temperature can be just as important as absolute temperatures.

May and June are, in some respects, the best months for ski touring. Easier road access to remote areas, long days, sunny skies, and delightful corn snow make longer, safe tours possible. Snow picnics become pleasant sojourns rather than races against hypothermia, and tours can take on a holiday air. Early May frequently has a major spring avalanche cycle, but by June the threat of avalanches is notably diminished, if not completely eliminated: Late-afternoon wet-snow sloughs must be considered, especially when it is very warm.

Dense wet-snow avalanches can travel for miles over very low-angle slopes (15 degrees) and are extremely dangerous. Time your ascent to take advantage of the sun's action: Climb when it's cool and make your descent just as the surface is soft and easy to ski, but before the snowpack is sodden or the surface frozen solid again later in the afternoon.

SOURCES OF WEATHER AND SNOW INFORMATION

Information about weather and snow can be obtained from a variety of public sources including newspapers, broadcast bulletins, special telephone services, and ski-shop bulletin boards.

Weather reports are broadcast by the National Weather Service at 162.55 Megahertz and may be received on inexpensive weather radios (the "crystal controlled" kind are the best) available at electronic hobby stores. Televised weather reports, depending on the TV station, are often quite complete and include the current weather situation, upper-level winds, the forecast, and sometimes even pass reports. The most important part of the televised report is the satellite photo and weather synopsis since from these you can estimate what mountain conditions will be.

Telephone and radio broadcast "ski reports" tend to be unreliably optimistic but do report 24-hour snowfall amounts and temperature variations between the various ski areas during the lift-served ski season.

Skiers may call AAA's Icicle Network at (206) 292-5385 for weather and highway information. Or, you may call the State Department of Highway's toll telephone number (1) 976-7623 for road conditions.

The USFS provides Backcountry and Avalanche Hazard Evaluation in a tape-recorded message at (206) 526-6677. In addition to describing avalanche potential for the region, this report is extremely valuable for determining what the snow conditions (the snowpack analysis) might be at a given location. This forecast is currently provided only through the winter season.

Large avalanches sometimes sweep the west slope of Boulder Pass — Tour 44 (Photo: Gary Brill).

All USFS and National Weather Service forecasts use the following terminology in describing avalanche hazard:

Low avalanche hazard. Mostly stable snow. Avalanches are unlikely except in isolated pockets on steep snow-covered open slopes and gullies. Backcountry travel is generally safe.

Moderate avalanche hazard. Areas of unstable snow. Avalanches are very possible on steep, snow-covered open slopes and gullies. Backcountry travelers should use caution.

High avalanche hazard. Mostly unstable snow. Avalanches are likely on steep, snow-covered open slopes and gullies. Backcountry travel is not recommended.

Extreme avalanche hazard. Widespread areas of unstable snow. Avalanches are certain on some steep snow-covered open slopes and gullies. Large destructive avalanches are possible. Backcountry travel should be avoided.

Skiers should know the meanings of these terms. Listen carefully to the report and take notes. This forecast is seasonal.

Perhaps the best source of information about skiing conditions is people who have just been there, including yourself. Keep in mind that conditions change rapidly: This morning's powder can turn to mush overnight. Keep a notebook of your tours, including location, weather, and snow conditions.

MOUNTAIN HAZARDS

Some of the tours described in this guide, indeed some of the best high routes in the Cascades, take place on glaciers and cliffy terrain. You must ski in complete control in these situations. Rope up when ascending active glaciers. Many skiers descend crevassed terrain without roping up, feeling that the bother of the rope forfeits any advantage obtained from its use. However, failure to carry adequate self-rescue equipment is irresponsible.

Crevasses often become bridged during storms that have high winds. This occurs frequently at higher elevations but has been observed as low as 6000 feet on the Easton Glacier. Skiing up with a rope is cheap insurance. If a tour requires a rope, it requires ice ax, prusik slings, and wands as well. Many spring tours require ice axes and crampons to negotiate short, steep sections safely.

Read *Mountaineering: The Freedom of the Hills,* and practice using your equipment in benign environments before an emergency. It's not the tools that protect you, it's their effective *use* that increases your security.

Glacier skiing is mountaineering and should be approached as such. Those not ready to travel in the glacial environment can still find superb off-glacier tours to very high places, such as the south-west shoulder of Mount Adams.

Mere snowfields and forests conceal hazards too. Forests with deep snowpacks develop tree wells, voids in the snow underneath the sheltering branches. A skier can fall into a tree well and be suspended upside down and helpless. Death by suffocation occurs in minutes. Anybody can fall into a tree well. The consequences need not be fatal if skiers use the buddy system. Always watch your partner ski (take pictures while you wait!) from a safe position. If there is trouble, you are then able to do something about it.

Moats often result when a deep snowpack creeps and melts away from an adjacent cliff. Skiing into a deep moat is similar to skiing off a cliff or into a crevasse. Moats are one reason that steep runs at ski areas are closed in late season. For example, the Trash Can run at Alpental gets notoriously cliffy in late season.

Whiteouts make even moderate slopes impossible to ski. They also make it impossible to identify hazardous snow or terrain conditions. When confronted by whiteout conditions proceed slowly and stay together until your party has descended beneath the clouds. Taking mental notes of local landmarks on the ascent helps you build a mental map of the route.

AVOIDING AVALANCHES

The best skiing takes place in avalanche terrain. To enjoy skiing safely, you must attempt to determine the chance of a slope sliding and what that event will mean to you. To acquire this skill, you should participate in avalanche safety courses. Check with moun-taineering shops for times and locations. Also read the "Recom-mended Reading" books about avalanche safety. Especially see Edward LaChapelle's *ABC of Avalanche Safety* and recall his words: "The only avalanche experts are dead."

Factors that affect the likelihood of avalanche include temperature and temperature change, precipitation, recent wind patterns, slope angle and curvature, the nature of the underlying terrain (grass vs. talus), and the nature of the snowpack itself.

Weather and Snow Factors

The Cascade ski season can be divided into three seasons to help in your analysis: early winter, midwinter, and spring. This does not apply to higher elevations on volcanoes, which experience a kind of winter throughout the entire year.

Avalanche potential is usually lower in early winter than in mid-

Unstable powder: Never do this. Heather Ridge —Tour 34 (Photo: Donal O'Sullivan).

winter since early in the season the snowpack is often anchored by terrain features such as stumps or talus. When these are covered by snow, it is midwinter for avalanche-prediction purposes.

Conditions, specific to the Cascades, that can result in unstable slopes include the following:

- A large storm with a warming trend results in extreme avalanche danger. Do not tour under these conditions.
- A cold storm with heavy snow and high winds results in deep slab formation on lee slopes and scoured snow on windward slopes. Skiing in trees is recommended since they help anchor the snowpack and often contain areas of light snow. The safest alternative is to go skiing in lift-served areas.
- A storm dumping cold snow on a hard-frozen crust decreases slope stability since there is little bonding between the frozen

crust and the cold snow. Contrast this with rain or wet snow falling on a crust: As the temperature gradually decreases and the precipitation continues, the slope becomes more stable as the crust refreezes.

- Cold snow building on buried surface hoar or a weak snow layer becomes increasingly unstable, especially on protected, north-facing slopes.
- A sudden midwinter warming trend sometimes destabilizes a recent heavy snowfall.
- Springtime warming trends cause snow sluffs and avalanches due to crust failures, lubrication of buried hard crusts, and general weakening of the snowpack due to warming (isothermal snowpack). The wet-snow avalanches that result can be extremely destructive because they can travel long distances and tend to be massive. This is most common in the afternoon and on south- and west-facing slopes.

Terrain Factors

Terrain must be considered when evaluating slope stability and route safety. Features that enhance stability include trees, talus, and stumps. Rocky-slab, grassy, or heather slopes present slippery surfaces to snow masses. For example, the southern slopes of Teebone Ridge (Tour 13) are grassy and extremely susceptible to sluffing, even with a thin snow cover. The presence of trees does not guarantee security; trees that are far enough apart to permit skiing are often far enough apart to permit avalanches to sweep through. For instance, the open trees on the southeastern slope of Heather Ridge (Tour 34) offer little resistance to powder-snow avalanches that sometimes occur here. Finally, the anchoring effect of rocks and stumps is reduced after the snowpack reaches a depth of a few feet.

The shape of a slope affects stability; convex slopes stretch the snowpack while concave slopes (progressively steeper uphill) compress the snowpack parallel to its surface. Loaded convex slopes are extremely dangerous because they tend to be more likely to release an avalanche than other slopes, and it is hard to predict where (or when) this will happen. For example, a convex slope may release suddenly when a skier is halfway down the hill. Small concave slopes are dangerous because a release could bury the skier on the gentler slope below. Slope size affects both avalanche potential and avalanche hazard: Large slopes tend to slide more easily, involve larger amounts of snow, and increase the risk to the skier.

Gullies should be considered "terrain traps" since they concentrate the destructive effects of even relatively small amounts of snow. Avoid them. Also avoid skiing directly below steep cliffs and large slopes that could dump snow on you. Skiers have been killed by being pinned against trees by snow slides. Cliffs present another risk: Even a small sluff could carry a skier over a cliff, with disastrous consequences.

Avalanche Survival

Tours in this guide are described as having Low, Moderate, or High avalanche *potential*. These descriptions refer to the terrain that skiers must cross to complete the tour. The categories are intended to be used in conjunction with USFS avalanche *hazard* evaluations. For example, a tour with Low avalanche potential can generally be safely skied in Low to Moderate avalanche hazard, while it should not be attempted in High avalanche hazard. Tours with Moderate avalanche potential can generally be done in Low avalanche hazard, but less often in Moderate avalanche hazard. Tours with High avalanche potential should only be attempted in conditions of Low avalanche hazard, or when the snowpack is well frozen.

Note the distinction between potential and hazard. Potential refers to the nature of the terrain while hazard refers to the USFS avalanche evaluation available from the forecast. Skiers should obtain an avalanche hazard evaluation before setting out. The avalanche potential categories in this guide apply only to the main route, not to side trips or extraordinary (but quite possible) conditions, such as deep instabilities, sudden weather changes, or terrain traps.

You can use the forecast to fine-tune your trips. If avalanche hazard is expected from accumulation of wind slab, pick a tour on windward slopes. If direct afternoon sun is expected to release wet snow slides, pick a north-facing tour (but beware of warming due to cloudy, hot weather). Build a base of experience to help you choose safe tours and try to anticipate unexpected hazards.

There are "safe harbors" in the mountains. The most efficient routes are often the safest. Ridge lines (avoid cornices) and wind-scoured or tree-covered slopes are generally safer than other areas. Benches are often more stable than adjacent steeper slopes. However, stay away from the uphill side of the bench. Also avoid slopes steeper than 30 degrees when avalanche hazard is above Low. When approaching a saddle or a ridge, avoid the slopes below cornices. If you must cross the avalanche starting zone, do so as high as possible. Keep to the flanks of slide paths. Generally it is safer to cross slide paths in the runout zone than in the starting zone. These are basic routefinding principles. Read the Recommended Reading books.

The most obvious warning sign of avalanche danger is present or recent avalanche activity. Other warning signs include large accumulations of new snow or high rates of snowfall (greater than an inch per hour), especially if accompanied by strong winds. Foot or ski penetration is a good measure of snow buildup. Gradually put your full body weight onto one foot or one ski: If your boot sinks 30 inches or more into the snow, danger is imminent (20 inches of penetration for the ski test). This test does not guarantee safety, but it does check snow settlement and the amount of snow available for avalanche.

Mid- and late-winter snowfalls often settle on top of hard rain or sun crusts, which present a smooth sliding surface. Snow buildups on such crusts, especially when poorly bonded, significantly increase avalanche hazard. Occasionally, if the underlying crust is weak, deeper avalanches can be released. In the absence of other warning signs on an unknown slope, try the inverted ski-pole test. Push the handle of your ski pole deep into the snow with a firm, smooth motion. As you penetrate the snow, feel for uneven resistance; this indicates crusts and weak layers. If you suspect these, you should dig a snow pit to evaluate slope stability. Snow-pit analysis is too technical to describe in a book of this nature. See Recommended Reading. Under the circumstances, if you have any doubt about a slope, go on to somewhere else. No ski run is worth your life.

Windward slopes are often scoured and hard surfaced. Lee slopes often develop windslab, a bonded mass of finely divided snow particles. Penetration tests may not work here. The slab may be either hard or soft, yet velvety looking, and sound hollow. (The north face of Jim Hill Mountain, Tour 37, often develops windslab). This is an extremely dangerous situation: When the weight of the slab or a skier causes the snowpack to fail, the entire slope will release simultaneously. Slabs triggered by skiers account for most avalanche fatalities. Prediction of slab release is uncertain at best. The most important question to ask is "What would happen if the slab released?"

Spring brings with it the safest touring conditions in the region. The snowpack has stabilized, and the main threats to skiers are avalanches caused by the weakening of crust layers due to rain or solar heating. Wet-snow slides can occur on slopes of any aspect and should be expected during sudden warm spells. May often has an active avalanche period resulting from the first extended warm-weather period. Avoid known avalanche areas during this time. Some areas, especially with shallow winter snowpacks, avalanche down to bare ground.

If you are caught in an avalanche, discard your skis and ski poles (if possible). Make swimming motions and try to stay on top of the moving snow. Work your way to the side of the avalanche. As you come to a stop, put one arm in front of your face to make an airspace in the snow and thrust the other arm up as high as possible to help rescuers locate you. If you are buried, remain calm. Do not fight the blackout. Remaining calm will help you live longer by conserving oxygen.

If you are a survivor, mark the place where you last saw the victim. Search for the victim directly downslope from the last known loca-

Frequently practice using your transceivers (Photo: Gary Brill).

tion. Look for a hand, ski, or bits of clothing. If the victim is not on the surface, use your transceiver to locate him. If you are not so equipped, probe the snow in a systematic fashion using probes or ski poles.

You are your friends' best hope for survival. Do not desert the victims and go for help, unless help is only a few minutes away. You must find them. Treat victims for suffocation and shock, as well as other suspected injuries.

Backcountry skiers must carry sufficient equipment to effect self-rescue. Avalanche transceivers, probes, and shovels are essential to safe winter touring. Take a class and read the suggested reading in this book to learn how to use these tools. Today's advanced rescue technology should not give you a sense of security: The fastest victim recovery does little good when the victim has already died of trauma suffered in the avalanche. In general, if there is doubt, don't go out. It just isn't worth it. Backcountry skiers cannot ski with the same sense of joyful abandon that patrolled-area skiers seem to enjoy, at least not in the long run. On the other hand, we are able to ski untracked snow for thousands of feet through astounding scenery.

*Moist marine air produces deep snowpacks; looking south from Mount Margaret —
Tour 53 (Photo: Joe Cattellani).*

Part II | Backcountry Tours

MOUNT BAKER HIGHWAY, STATE ROUTE 542

The Mount Baker Highway runs through to ski country with European-style mountain views and snow depths often exceeding 10 feet. While the deep snow accumulations extend the season well into summer, they also carry with them high avalanche danger in the winter. Some tours in this area are safe only when the snowpack is well frozen; that is early in the morning in the spring. The weather is sometimes good, especially when a low-pressure system passes to the southeast, under convergence conditions to the south, or when high pressure is building from the northwest. When the visibility is good, the views are breath-taking. The grandeur of hanging glaciers, jagged mountains, remote ski runs, and better snow conditions makes this region attractive.

The main watercourse in this area is the Nooksack River, which springs from the mighty glaciers on the north side of Mount Shuksan. The Mount Baker Highway follows the river, then climbs to the Mount Baker ski area (eight miles northeast of the volcano). Many of the tours start low in valleys adjacent to the highway and require substantial climbs to get to the skiing. Side roads are generally unmaintained in winter and snow-covered until mid-April. Most of the tours terminate above treeline and are not worthwhile except in good weather.

The town of Glacier is the last population center before the highway climbs to snowline. Food and refreshments are available at local stores and restaurants. The ranger station just east of town is a source of snow and weather information.

Because many of the Nooksack tours traverse known avalanche areas, it is essential to review weather forecasts before setting out: A storm with a warming trend could trap your party until sliding slopes have stabilized.

CHOWDER RIDGE

1

Start Point	Wells Creek Roadhead, No. 403, 4700 feet
High Point	Hadley Peak, 7515 feet
Best Time	July to November
Length	Day trip; 10 miles; 8 to 12 hours
Difficulty	Intermediate; some glacier skiing; low avalanche potential
Maps	Green Trails No. 13, Mount Baker; USGS 15-minute series, Mount Baker

Chowder Ridge affords excellent early- and late-season skiing over moderate terrain. In good weather, spectacular views of Mount Baker, Shuksan, and the American Border Peaks add to the experience. This is a summer and fall tour because access becomes more difficult once the road is snow-covered. The snow cover lasts well into summer.

Drive Mount Baker Highway (State Route 542) east from Glacier for 8 miles. Just past the Nooksack Power Plant, turn right onto Wells Creek road. After crossing the Nooksack River, drive 1.5 miles and turn right at the first fork.

The Wells Creek road parallels the creek for about 2 miles past the fork (4 miles past the Nooksack crossing). Five miles from the Nooksack crossing, the road crosses Wells Creek and follows Bar Creek for 1 mile, then winds uphill toward the crest of Cougar Divide. Continue driving as far as conditions permit, possibly parking in a clearcut at the ridge crest (4700 feet).

Hike or ski south along the open crest (huckleberry bushes in summer) toward the big white lump on the southern horizon. The views from this area of the American Border Peaks, Shuksan, and Baker are stunning.

Continue skiing southwest along the broad crest of Cougar Divide (5000 feet and higher). Small (50 feet) lava cliffs near the crest are bypassed on the east (left) side. Chowder Ridge (about 7000 feet) lies 3 miles to the southwest. If you decide to turn around here, you can take good runs from Cougar Divide, especially to the east.

If you decide to continue, a good objective is Hadley Peak, the

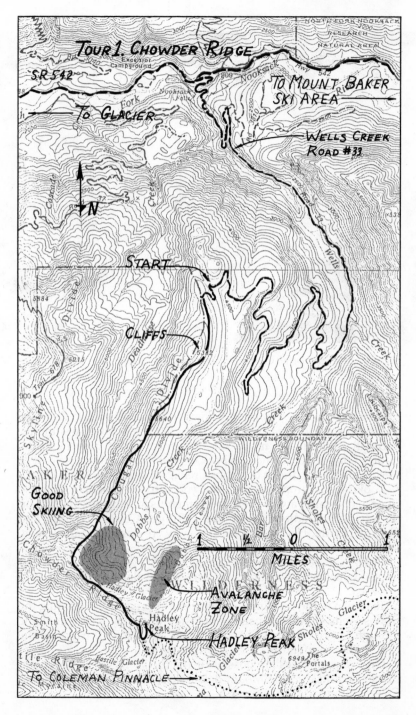

TOUR 1. CHOWDER RIDGE

S.R. 542

TO GLACIER

TO MOUNT BAKER SKI AREA

WELLS CREEK ROAD #33

START

CLIFFS

GOOD SKIING

AVALANCHE ZONE

HADLEY PEAK

TO COLEMAN PINNACLE

1   ½   0   1
MILES

Traversing Hadley Glacier; Cougar Divide in the background (Photo: Gary Brill).

eastern end and high point of Chowder Ridge. Climb Hadley from the south side, leaving your skis 200 to 300 feet below the summit.

Small cliffs on the north side prevent a direct descent to the Hadley Glacier, so downclimb back to your skis and traverse east or west. This glacier drains to Dobbs Creek, a tributary to Wells Creek.

Looking east from Hadley Peak you can see Coleman Pinnacle (Tour 5) one valley away. There are numerous touring possibilities on the alp slopes adjoining Chowder Ridge, Cougar Divide, and Skyline Divide. Hadley Glacier is heavily crevassed and unsuitable for skiing except in spring and early summer.

Dobbs Cleaver (the north ridge of Hadley Peak) joins very steep slopes, which are likely areas for large slab avalanches. Stay clear of this area.

To return to the car, simply reverse the approach. Descending the Dobbs-Wells Creek drainage is untested and may result in skiing through heavy timber and brush. There are also cliff bands to the east. Allow enough time for a daylight ski to the car.

One-way traverses are possible using the Wells Creek approach. Parties could ski to the Mount Baker ski area via Hadley Peak and Coleman Pinnacle, or vice versa.

RUTH MOUNTAIN

2

	Start Point	Hannegan Campground, 3100 feet
	High Point	Ruth Mountain, 7106 feet; or Icy Peak, 7070 feet
	Best Time	April to July
	Length	Day trip to Mount Ruth; 12 miles; 9 to 12 hours
		Day trip to Icy Peak; 15 miles; 11 to 14 hours
	Difficulty	Advanced; glacier travel; navigation; high avalanche potential
Map—page 38	**Maps**	Green Trails No. 14, Mount Shuksan; USGS 15-minute series, Mount Shuksan

Ruth Mountain is a magnificent ski touring objective. Of moderate elevation, its white bulk overlooks rugged Nooksack Cirque and the spectacular Pickett Range. The peak is reached via Ruth Creek and Hannegan Pass.

Ruth Creek lies in a deep gorge, headed at the east end by the bulk of Ruth Mountain. Virtually the entire approach is exposed to large avalanche slopes beginning 3000 to 4000 feet above the trail. This makes avalanche-hazard evaluation virtually meaningless for this

Descending to Ruth Creek; note the avalanche debris (Photo: Gary Brill).

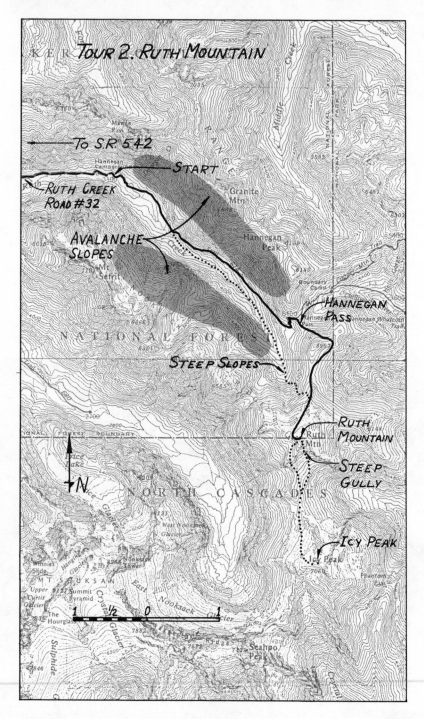

TOUR 2. RUTH MOUNTAIN

To S.R 542

START

RUTH CREEK
ROAD #32

Granite
Mtn

AVALANCHE
SLOPES

Hannegan
Peak

HANNEGAN
PASS

NATIONAL FOREST

STEEP SLOPES

RUTH
MOUNTAIN

Ruth
Mtn

STEEP
GULLY

N

NORTH CASCADES

ICY PEAK

Icy Peak

MT. SHUKSAN

1   ½   0   1

approach route. This tour should be attempted only by very strong parties in ideal conditions; that is, when the snowpack is well frozen.

Drive the Mount Baker Highway 12.8 miles past the town of Glacier. Just before the Nooksack River Bridge, turn left on Nooksack River road No. 32. Drive 1.5 miles and take the left-forking Ruth Creek road and drive as far as conditions permit. Road end, and Hannegan Campground, is at 3100 feet, 4.5 miles from the highway. If road conditions prevent driving to the end of the road, ski the road to the trailhead. Hike or ski the trail on the north side of Ruth Creek. The trail is usually snow covered until May.

For the first mile, the trail meanders southeast along the gently sloping valley floor. Then it begins a climbing traverse, with the last mile climbing steeply (4+ switchbacks, 1000 feet) through forest to Hannegan Pass (5066 feet). Total elevation gain from trailhead to pass is 2000 feet.

Looking east from Hannegan Pass, you see the Chilliwack drainage and Copper Peak. Ski east, then make a southward (right) traverse from the pass, below cliffs (right). Ascend the east slope of the north ridge to the broad north shoulder of Ruth Mountain. Continue south 1 mile to Ruth Glacier. Ascend the glacier. As you approach the false summit, skirt around its west side. Avoid crevasses that may lurk here. The true summit becomes apparent and is gained easily.

An alternative, more direct approach to Ruth Mountain crosses Ruth Creek over avalanche debris while still low in the valley, then makes a climbing traverse directly toward the Peak. Continue nearly to the head of Ruth Creek before ascending a steep headwall (cliff bands) about 800 feet to gain the saddle between Point 5963 and Ruth Mountain. Continue according to the regular route instructions. Descend by skiing directly to the Ruth Creek drainage, if conditions permit.

Icy Peak lies south of Ruth Mountain; make a descending traverse around the west side of Ruth, dropping to 5600 feet before climbing to the Ruth–Icy saddle.

From the saddle, traverse the west side of Icy Peak to ascend its southwest shoulder. Or, descend from the summit of Ruth toward the southeast, removing skis to negotiate a steep gully. From the bench at the bottom of the gully, head southwest toward the saddle between Ruth and Icy and ascend the normal route. The skiing is moderate except for the steep gullies leading to the Ruth–Icy saddle. This side trip takes another 3 to 4 hours. Return to the car via Ruth Mountain.

Remember that the descent from Hannegan Pass is steep and should be done in daylight. To complicate matters, late-afternoon sun often causes wet snow slides below the pass. A warming trend or warm daytime temperatures could trigger deep releases of the snowpack. Under such conditions, it may be better to wait until *after* the sun leaves these slopes to allow them to stabilize. Crampons and ice axes are recommended for this tour.

Hannegan Pass is also the entry point for a ski traverse of the Pickett Range and other high routes. This range's rugged scenery is unsurpassed.

SHUKSAN ARM

3

Start Point	Mount Baker Ski Area, 4240 feet
High Point	Shuksan Arm, 5540 feet
Best Time	November to April
Length	Half-day trip; 1 mile; 1 to 4 hours, more depending on side trips
Difficulty	Advanced; high avalanche potential; should not be attempted in whiteout
Maps	Green Trails No. 14, Mount Shuksan; USGS 15-minute series, Mount Shuksan

Most ski areas in Washington State don't give the skier a real alpine feeling, that sense of being in the high mountains. Mount Baker's ski area is the exception. By ascending Shuksan Arm, a long, glaciated outrigger of Mount Shuksan itself, the backcountry skier can experience that sense of "being in the high mountains" within an hour of civilization. Chair lifts are planned for this area within the next two years—enjoy the solitude while you can.

On top of Shuksan Arm (Photo: Gary Brill).

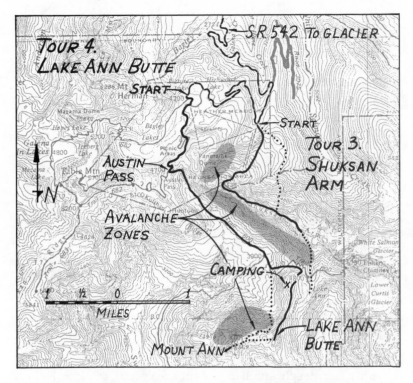

From the Mount Baker ski area parking lot ride the Shuksan Arm lifts (number 4 or 5) or climb gentler slopes to the east to the upper terminal (4900 feet). Climb the hill behind (southwest of) the station for 0.4 mile until you arrive at the western end of Shuksan Arm (5540 feet). This hill often develops steep and wind-loaded "rolls." If you suspect wind loading, abandon the tour: Avalanche deaths have occurred here.

Reduced-visibility conditions make it impossible to determine slope conditions — don't go here in foggy weather. From this knoll, you can descend northwest to the Panorama Dome area, ski back down the hill toward the lift towers (northeast), or traverse left (southeast) along the crest of Shuksan Arm. You'll be able to ski along the ridge for more than a mile before towers and cliffs block further progress. The proximity of the wintry northwest side of Shuksan is awesome and provides a good backdrop for a lunch stop.

The easiest descent involves retracing your tracks to the knoll at the west end of Shuksan Arm and descending through or adjacent to the ski area. In safe conditions, ski northeast of the Shuksan Arm chair, remaining on the Mount Shuksan side. Descend just right of a gully next to the ski area. Ski to about 4200 feet, then climb out of a gully and return to the ski area.

Skiers should take full touring and navigation equipment and should allow enough time to make the tour in daylight. Whiteout conditions or poor lighting may make recognition of avalanche slopes difficult in this area: Steep, rolling terrain and the lack of natural anchors make this a hazardous area.

LAKE ANN BUTTE

4

Map — page 41

Start Point	Mount Baker Ski Area, 4200 feet
High Point	Lake Ann Butte, 5800 feet
Best Time	December to April
Length	Day trip or excellent overnight; 9 miles; 6 to 8 hours
Difficulty	Advanced; moderate avalanche potential
Maps	Green Trails No. 14, Mount Shuksan; USGS 15-minute series, Mount Shuksan

This tour offers easy access to unusual winter views of Mounts Shuksan and Baker. While this tour is a reasonable day trip, it is more fun as an overnighter because of all the skiing to be had near Lake Ann. Stable conditions are essential to safe completion of this tour. Do not attempt it in warm weather or with the threat of rain.

From the Mount Baker ski area, follow the Austin Pass road past the Austin run. It is faster to ski this than it is to ride the lift. Just past the run, climb steeply uphill to rejoin the road 400 feet above. Follow the road to Austin Pass and descend a gladed slope, losing 400 feet, to upper Swift Creek valley. Shuksan Arm now looms immediately to the northeast.

Ski southeast for 0.8 mile through open glades along the center of the valley. Avalanche slopes rise on either side. It is best to stay east (left) of Swift Creek to avoid problems in crossing it lower down.

Soon the flat valley bottom begins to steepen. Enter the forest on the left, traversing southeast and descending slightly to avoid steeper slopes above. In 1 mile you'll break out of the forest. Stay on the north side of the creek coming from the vicinity of Lake Ann. Climb to the saddle near the outlet of the lake. It lies just over the saddle at 4800 feet. Careful routefinding is required on the climb to the saddle to minimize danger from avalanche tracks.

Lake Ann Butte's southeast peak is a good goal. To reach the peak, climb from the 4800-foot saddle along the ridge that lies due west of the lake. Ski the ridge on or near its crest, avoiding cornices. Traverse on an intricate series of benches on the southeast side of the ridge. Once past the false summit, climb steeply to the crest. The southeast peak is an easy tour up the ridge from here (0.2 mile to the south).

It is possible to reach the true summit of Lake Ann Butte by rounding the southeast summit and following the ridge crest west

Mount Shuksan from Lake Ann Butte (Photo: Gary Brill).

for 0.5 mile. This sidetrip takes about 3 hours and involves some steep skiing. It is easier to reach the summit by turning off (southwest) from the Lake Ann approach before starting the climb up to Lake Ann. This is a very steep ascent.

Reverse the approach to escape to the car. If you decide to make this an overnight tour, be sure to make overnight parking arrangements with the ski-area management. This tour has fantastic views and numerous good ski runs.

COLEMAN PINNACLE

5

Map—
page 46

Start Point	Mount Baker Ski Lodge, 4240 feet
High Point	Coleman Pinnacle, 6414 feet
Best Time	October to June
Length	Day trip; 9 miles; 6 to 10 hours
Difficulty	Intermediate; high avalanche potential
Maps	Green Trails No. 14, Mount Shuksan; USGS 15-minute series, Mount Shuksan

Coleman Pinnacle is distinguished for its occasional views of nearby Mount Baker and the miles of untracked powder it offers to early-season visitors. Navigation skills are essential for this tour due to occasional whiteouts, and avalanche hazard is a major factor in limiting this tour. Check with the snow ranger and don't hesitate to change objectives if the hazard is anything but low.

From the Mount Baker ski area, follow the Austin Pass road past the Austin run. It is faster to ski this than it is to ride the lift. Just past the run, climb steeply uphill to rejoin the road 400 feet above. Follow the road until it begins to head southeast toward Artist Point (Huntoon Point on 1953 USGS map). Climb southwest here for 200 feet to regain the road near its end. By now you should be at the large, nearly level area beneath Table Mountain.

From here, traverse west for 0.8 mile, beneath the steep south face of Table Mountain. Maintain a constant elevation of 5000 feet. The south face of Table Mountain is a very dangerous avalanche slope: Even a slight warming trend may release major slides (as early as October).

From the saddle southwest of Table Mountain, Ptarmigan Ridge, the long ridge connecting to Coleman Pinnacle, becomes obvious. There are two approaches to Coleman Pinnacle. A short but dangerous traverse from the saddle across a steep and often wind-loaded slope leads to lower angle slopes below Ptarmigan Ridge. After reaching a level area on the crest, stay mostly on the crest or slightly south as you traverse (the north side is generally heavily corniced).

If the steep slope of this approach lacks appeal, drop a few

Coleman Pinnacle and distant Mount Baker from Ptarmigan Ridge (Photo: Gary Brill).

hundred feet to the north and traverse well below steep slopes to the lower angled névé below Coleman Pinnacle. Climb these slopes to get to the Pinnacle. The Pinnacle can also be approached via Herman Saddle and the Chain Lakes. This approach has more up and down than the other routes but offers less avalanche hazard than the south side of Table Mountain.

Whether or not you decide to reach Coleman Pinnacle, there are abundant possibilities for runs over 2000 feet in length. Return via the approach, remembering the possible effects of sun on snow-laden slopes.

A good high route is a traverse past Coleman Pinnacle to Chowder Ridge and Wells Creek. This traverse takes two to three days in good conditions.

SHOLES GLACIER

6

Start Point	Mount Baker Ski Area, 4200 feet
High Point	The Portals, 6200 feet
Best Time	April to October
Length	Overnight; 16 miles; 14 hours
Difficulty	Intermediate; high avalanche potential; navigation; optional glacier skiing
Maps	Green Trails Nos. 13 and 14, Mounts Baker and Shuksan; USGS 15-minute series, Mounts Baker and Shuksan

In good weather, Sholes Glacier offers the quintessential summer tour: Warm temperatures, green meadows, sprays of alpine flowers,

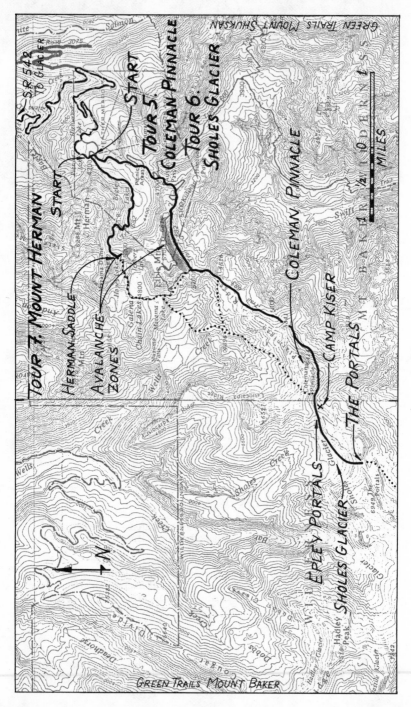

mountain goats, and great corn snow skiing. This tour provides access to a seldom visited side of Mount Baker.

Sholes Glacier can be seen as a logical extension of the Coleman Pinnacle Tour (No. 5). Sholes Glacier is a distinct tour since its objectives, range, and season are significantly different than the Coleman Pinnacle trip.

Hike or ski southwest from the Mount Baker lodge to Coleman Pinnacle. The last half of the trail, often snow-covered until mid-August, lies on the south side of Ptarmigan Ridge.

Past the Pinnacle (west and south) 0.3 mile is a broad saddle (Camp Kiser, 5 miles, 5840 feet) where you can make camp. Ski west from Camp Kiser to Epley Portals (about 6000 feet), a shallow saddle which opens west on to the gently sloping Sholes Glacier. Once over the saddle, continue skiing left (southwest) along the south side of the Sholes Glacier to The Portals, a broad saddle (6200 feet) 0.5 mile east of Peak 6949 on Landes Cleaver.

From The Portals you can take runs to the south on the Rainbow Glacier or to the north on the Portals Glacier. Be aware that there are crevasses on both — wands may be useful for marking crossing. Return via the route of ascent.

This tour could be the beginning of a traverse over the summit of Mount Baker. Parties have made the traverse in 3 days, but it is a mountaineering tour.

To start the tour, ski south through The Portals. Make a southwest-trending climb of the Rainbow Glacier below Landes Cleaver but above icefalls on the Rainbow. Continue the climbing traverse to the Boulder Glacier (due east of the summit) to avoid the Park Glacier headwall. Ascend Boulder Glacier to reach the summit and descend via the Roman Wall to Heliotrope Ridge.

There are definite avalanche and crevasse hazards on this tour. See Fred Beckey's *Cascade Alpine Guide*, vol. 3 for details.

MOUNT HERMAN

7

Start Point	Mount Baker Ski Area, 4200 feet
High Point	Herman Saddle, 5300 feet
Best Time	November to March
Length	Day trip; 5 miles; 2 to 3 hours
Difficulty	Intermediate; moderate avalanche potential
Maps	Green Trails No. 14, Mount Shuksan; USGS 15-minute series, Mount Shuksan

Herman Saddle lies just north of Table Mountain. This short tour doesn't actually climb the peak. Rather, it brings the skier to Herman Saddle just southwest of Mount Herman and offers unbroken open slopes, fine skiing, and a change of scenery from the grand-scale views of the Shuksan area. This tour is best done with only small amounts of new snow.

From the Mount Baker lodge head south across the valley toward and past the Forest Service building. Just beyond the structure, begin to head west alongside Bagley Lakes. Stay away from the steep slopes beneath Table Mountain (slab avalanches) and be aware of wet snow avalanches off Mount Herman to the north, especially in the afternoon.

Make a climbing traverse west until you are due north of the east end of Table Mountain. Climb the steepening hill (northwest) to gain 800 feet in 0.3 mile, keeping to the right (north) side of the basin until the slope angle eases off (near 5200 feet).

Head southwest toward Herman Saddle, passing tree-covered Mazama Dome on its left side (to your right). A good lunch spot can be found in trees near the saddle (5300 feet).

Return by reversing the ascent route or skiing around Table Mountain (3 additional miles, navigation). If you descend the approach route from Herman Saddle, follow your tracks north for the first 0.3 mile before skiing down, thus avoiding the cliffs below Table Mountain.

Climbing Bagley Peak; Table Mountain lies in the immediate background (Photo: Gary Brill).

Coleman and Roosevelt glaciers seen from Heliotrope Ridge (Photo: Gary Brill).

COLEMAN GLACIER

8

Map — page 50

Start Point	Heliotrope Ridge Trailhead, 3700 feet
High Point	Coleman Glacier, 7000 feet
Best Time	October to November, April to June
Length	Day trip or good overnight; 9 miles; 7 to 10 hours
Difficulty	Advanced; glacier skiing; moderate avalanche potential
Maps	Green Trails No. 13, Mount Baker; USGS 15-minute series, Mount Baker

The Coleman Glacier on Mount Baker contrasts a remote alpine environment with sunset views of the San Juan Islands and the Strait of Juan de Fuca. This tour, which follows the first part of the classic summit route, offers glacier skiing on the northwest side of our northernmost volcano.

Past the town of Glacier 0.7 mile is the Glacier Creek road (No. 39). Ignore the two side roads that join the Glacier Creek road in the first mile. Follow the main road past Coal Creek (5 miles) to an intersection (5.4 miles from highway). Take the right road (left is abandoned and overgrown) and continue to another fork. Take the left, about 8.5 miles from the highway, to the trailhead.

The trail dips into the forest at the eastern edge of the parking lot and is obvious even when snow covered. Metal markers help show the way to the former site of Kulshan Cabin (2 miles, 4700 feet). The historic building was demolished in 1986 because it had fallen into disrepair.

Continue climbing east-southeast from the cabin site, breaking out of the trees near 5200 feet. If you decide to make this an overnight tour, this is a good place to camp. The best early-season skiing is found on Heliotrope Ridge, just above this area, but below 6200 feet. Ascend the slope south of the campsite, bearing slightly east until you reach a broad bench. Head west along this bench until the bowls become obvious at your feet (1 mile). Wind-loading can turn these

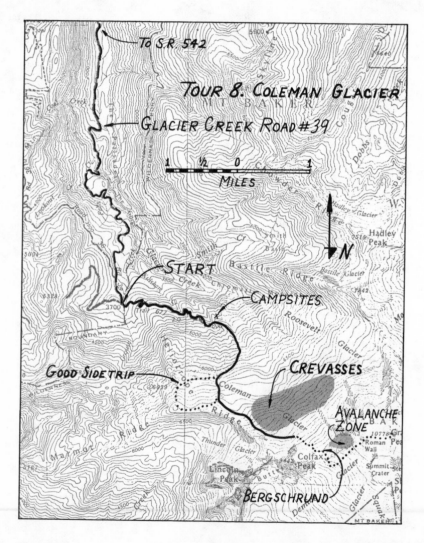

bowls and the glacier above into traps. The glacier should be avoided in the late fall because crevasses may be thinly bridged.

A good spring tour objective is the junction of Heliotrope and Marmot ridges, at about 7000 feet. Scenic camp and bivouac sites abound and good views of the Black Buttes, the Coleman headwall, and the San Juan Islands can be had in good weather conditions.

From the campsite, head south and climb the open slope to the broad bench at about 6000 feet. The lower glacier is usually crevassed. Many skiers take wands to mark crevasse hazards. Continue climbing, southeast now, until you approach the crest of Heliotrope Ridge (from 7000 to 7500 feet). Maintain a high traverse to keep away from crevasses on the lower Coleman Glacier.

Make camp at some pleasant flat spot on the ridge crest, or return from here. Overnighters may wish to ski higher on the Coleman Glacier, perhaps even to the summit. The crevasses on this glacier are huge and have swallowed climbers before. Rope up and use prusiks while making the ascent. Descend by retracing the route of ascent.

This area experienced much ablation in 1985 and may not be suitable for skiing after late spring unless it receives considerable snowfall the next few winters.

NORTH CASCADES HIGHWAY, STATE ROUTE 20

The successful completion and maintenance of the North Cascades Highway (State Route 20) has created year-around access to much of the terrain along the highway corridor. Even though the highway is closed by late November, it is driveable to Diablo Lake year around — many of the tours in this area start before the road gate.

Touring in this area requires navigation skills as well as acute sensitivity to snow stability. The early-season snowpack sometimes covers the infamous North Cascades brush. You can then ski right over it. In any case, tours in this area require stamina and a sense of adventure because of their typical large elevation gain and their remoteness.

State Route 20 heads east from the town of Mount Vernon, past the western sentinel of Sauk Mountain near Rockport. The highway parallels the Skagit Eagle Preserve. Alert watchers can sometimes see bald eagles fishing the Skagit between Rockport and Marblemount.

The town of Marblemount is the last fuel and food stop before Mazama, on the other side of the range. Here the Cascade River meets the Skagit and skiers obtain access to Teebone Ridge, Eldorado, and the Cascade Pass area.

Many tours in this area take place within national park areas. Backcountry permits, which may be obtained from the National Park Service, are required for overnight tours. These are available at NPS ranger stations located near Marblemount and Winthrop, or by mail. The Marblemount ranger station is situated one mile west of town. If you are coming from east of the crest, obtain your permits at the NPS ranger station in Winthrop. High-use areas are booked up months in advance. Either plan ahead or have alternative plans in case you cannot obtain a permit for your area of choice.

Some excellent skiing objectives in the region, not described in this guide, lie east of Silver Star Mountain. Tours taken from Harts Pass and Methow Valley tours, especially Fawn Peak and Robinson Peak, provide very fine, long runs with overnight access. Other touring possibilities include Buck Mountain, Oval Peak, Reynolds Peak, Abernathy Peak, and Big Craggy. There are numerous tours in the Pasayten Wilderness Area, especially in the Remmel Mountain-Cathedral Peak area. Cutthroat Peak and Sandy Butte are easily accessible from Route 20. Some of these tours (and many others) are described in Sally Portman's excellent *Ski Touring Methow Style*.

SILVER STAR MOUNTAIN

9

Start Point	Silver Star Creek, 4200 feet
High Point	Saddle between East and West Summits, 8600 feet
Best Time	April to May, immediately after the highway opens
Length	Overnight; 8 miles; 10 hours
Difficulty	Advanced; glacier travel; moderate avalanche potential
Maps	Green Trails No. 50, Washington Pass; USGS 7.5-minute series, Silver Star

The skiing doesn't get any better than this. A long run among huge granitic towers and larches, often in deep powder, and relatively easy access make Silver Star a worthy objective. Avalanche hazard must be considered on this tour. Silver Star Creek valley and slopes directly below the summit saddle often get loaded by prevailing winds. Any significant depth of new, unsettled snow on the gently sloping glacier below the final headwall indicates a high avalanche risk and the need to turn back: Windslabs below the 8600-foot col could release from above you as you climb. Silver Star is

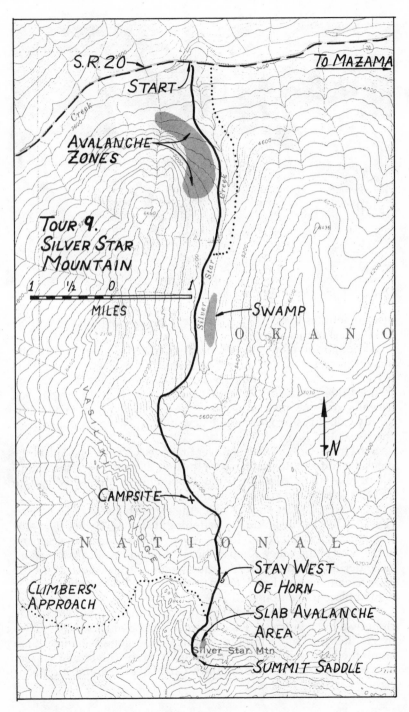

S.R. 20 → · · · · · · · · · · · To Mazama

Start

Avalanche Zones

Tour 9.
Silver Star Mountain

1   ½   0   1
MILES

Swamp

O K A N O

N

National

Campsite

Climbers' Approach

Stay West Of Horn

Slab Avalanche Area

Silver Star Mtn

Summit Saddle

Descending Silver Star Creek on spring corn (Photo: Gary Brill).

also sometimes invaded by helicopter skiers, lessening the wilderness aspect of this tour.

Although there are two climbing approaches, only one is really suitable for a ski ascent: Silver Star Creek basin. This route ascends Silver Star Creek (7.5 miles west of Early Winters Information Center) due south to the Silver Star Glacier. The other approach ascends Willow Creek and enters the Silver Star Glacier via Burgundy Col. It is steep, frequently icy, and tends to melt out early in the season.

Start from the west side of Silver Star Creek. (The east bank of the creek may offer better traveling for the first 800 feet of elevation gain.) Ski or hike south, climbing through open forest and keeping 100 to 200 feet west of the gullied streambed.

At about 4300 feet and 0.7 mile, the slope steepens and climbs a steep 400 feet before gradually flattening at about 4700 feet. The next mile, through mostly open forest, leads you to an avalanche clearing at the head of the valley. Keep to the right here to avoid a swamp and meandering stream. A steep cirque looms ahead. Pass this on the right to gain the next bench (6400 feet). The right side of this bench is a good place for camping.

Ski due south toward the steep headwall that is bounded on the right by a huge buttress. The headwall is divided into three gullies by granite ribs. Take a minute to evaluate the slope's stability, then climb the headwall via the leftmost gully to the Silver Star Glacier above. The Wine Spires (Burgundy, Chablis, etc.) are now on your right.

Ski up the left side of the glacier until you approach the steep slopes below the final col. At that point make a climbing traverse right, then ski to the saddle (8600 feet). The true summit lies to the east of the col; an easy 15-minute climb with an ice ax affords spectacular views.

Return via the approach. In early season, it is possible to ski all the way back to the car, a run of over 4000 vertical feet.

EARLY WINTERS SPIRES

10

Start Point	Blue Lake Trailhead, 5280 feet
High Point	Early Winters-Blue Peak Notch, 7600 feet
Best Time	April to June, immediately after the highway opens
Length	Overnight; 8 miles; 7 hours
Difficulty	Intermediate; moderate avalanche potential
Maps	Green Trails Nos. 50 and 82, Washington Pass and Stehekin; USGS 7.5-minute series, Washington Pass

Map—
page 56

Powder skiing among larches and unusual views of Liberty Bell are among the potential pleasures of this tour. The good weather associated with the eastern slope of the Cascades doesn't hurt either.

Park at the Blue Lake trailhead about 1.2 miles west of Washington Pass. In early season it's easier to ski directly southeast from the highway toward Blue Peak, passing left of a swampy area. In about

Bowls west of Liberty Bell (Photo: Brian Sullivan).

0.3 mile, you'll come to a large avalanche path. Follow the snow and debris to a steep headwall at 6200 feet, then pass it by a gully on the right side. Work up and left on open slopes and benches, then climb right to a notch at 7600 feet, 0.3 mile south of South Early Winters Spire.

From the notch you have a number of choices: Camp here and ski the slopes above the highway; descend the east side of the Early Winters massif and ski a narrow gully to the hairpin turn in State Route 20; or climb to the crest above, staying left of the huge and dangerous cornice on Blue Peak. Considerable avalanche debris is found on the slopes beneath the 20- to 40-foot cornice, evidence of its activity.

There are many days of skiing available in this vicinity, much of it very good and relatively safe. One option is the "Birthday Tour," an excellent day trip traversing Blue Peak Col, Copper Creek, and Kangaroo Pass to the hairpin curve on Route 20. See Sally Portman's *Ski Touring Methow Style* for a good description of this route. The fairly steep northwest slopes of Early Winters Spires also offer a fine tour. It would take a lot of weekends to thoroughly explore the many touring options in this area.

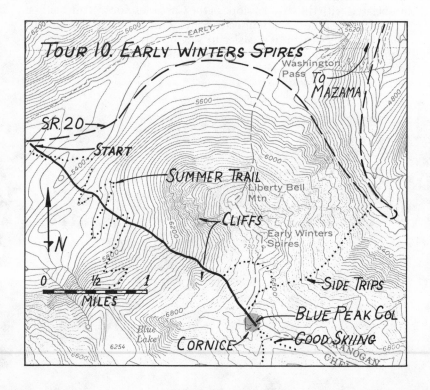

BLACK PEAK

11

Start Point	Rainy Pass, 4800 feet	
High Point	South Ridge of Black Peak, 8000 feet; or Black Peak Summit, 8970 feet	
Best Time	April to July, immediately after the highway opens	
Length	Overnight; 10 miles; 7 hours	
Difficulty	Advanced; steep snow; moderate avalanche potential	
Maps	Green Trails Nos. 49 and 50, Mount Logan and Washington Pass; USGS 7.5-minute series, Mount Arriva and Rainy Pass	

*Map—
page 58*

Rainy Pass is the entry point for a number of major tours accessible from the North Cascades Highway. This area is far enough east to offer an alternative to west-side tours made risky due to bad weather. Weak fronts sometimes fail to penetrate as far east as Rainy Pass, and skiers can make successful tours even while the Cascade Pass area farther west is receiving rain. This tour is an intricate traverse over connected double cirques. Skiers attempting this tour should be competent at self-arrest on steep slopes, since some of the traverses are quite exposed. A slip could put you over a cliff.

Park your car at Rainy Pass on the west side of State Route 20. The approach to Black Peak is made via the Lake Ann trail, probably snow covered during the touring season.

The trail begins 0.2 mile west of Rainy Pass and heads southwest, gaining 500 feet in 0.5 mile through deep forest.

Soon the trail makes a left turn and, in 0.1 mile, a right to traverse below a rib and enter the basin containing Lake Ann. A junction is 1.5 miles from the road. Take the right fork and begin a 1.5-mile ascent to Heather Pass (6050 feet). If the trail is not visible, simply begin a climbing traverse above Lake Ann, heading toward Heather Pass. This slope is quite steep: The main dangers are from possible slips on the steep, often icy, slope or sluffs as the hill warms under the morning sun.

Heather Pass is a great place for lunch or camping should you decide to stop here. While you're relaxing, look west to see the next leg of the tour. The route heads due west from Heather Pass. A slight descent, then a 2-mile traverse over steep, undulating terrain takes you to Wing Lake and your campsite. To get there requires the crossing of at least one steep and exposed chute.

Your inspection should take in the size of the cornices drooping from the ridge above the route (on your left). Consider the temperature and how fast your party is moving as well. If, in your judgment, the cornices look precipitous, consider Heather Pass the high point of the tour. (A good alternative plan is to follow the ridge from Heather

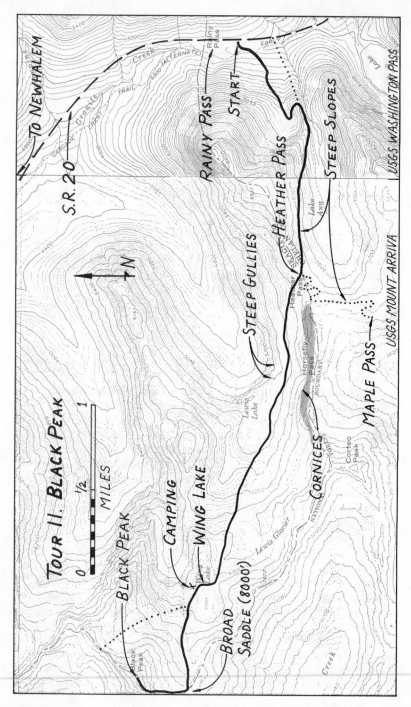

TOUR II. BLACK PEAK

The route to Black Peak (Photo: Brian Sullivan).

Pass west to Point 6870, then to Maple Pass, staying south of the ridge.)

Continuing from Heather Pass to Wing Lake, descend from the saddle and scurry above Lewis Lake to the moraine west and behind it. Lewis Lake will probably be frozen. Climb the moraine west of the lake, giving wide berth to the cliffs on your left. In less than a mile and 1000 feet you will reach the Wing Lake basin (6900 feet). A good camp can be made on a bench just north of the outlet.

The most reasonable approach to the summit of Black Peak is via its south shoulder. Hike counterclockwise around the east end of Wing Lake to avoid cliffs on the west side. Once northwest of the lake, climb the snowfield west to the col on Black Peak's southern shoulder. An ice ax is often necessary, as the last few hundred feet below the 8000-foot col are quite steep and usually overhung by a cornice. Watch for signs of slab formation. Sometimes the talus slopes on your right (north) may offer an easier ascent to the notch. Leave your skis at the pass for the summit climb (class 3, some exposure).

The descent to Wing Lake faces due east, so time your run accordingly. Another good run descends from the col (about 8200 feet) just east of Black Peak. There is a small, stagnant icefield on this slope, but it is usually covered by snow and is often good for skiing.

To return, simply retrace your tracks, observing even greater caution. If you lose the trail below Lake Ann, descend east. Rainy Pass will be on your left when you reach the highway. Allow plenty of time to get to the car before dark.

SNOWFIELD PEAK

12

Start Point	Pyramid Lake Trailhead, 1150 feet
High Point	Colonial–Neve Col, 6840 feet
Best Time	March to June
Length	Overnight; 11 miles; 9 hours
Difficulty	Advanced; high avalanche potential; possible bushwhack; small snowshoes useful
Maps	Green Trails No. 48, Diablo Dam; USGS 7.5-minute series, Diablo Dam and Ross Lake

This tour is accessible all year since State Route 20 is almost always open to Thunder Arm. Both the Neve and the Colonial glaciers offer excellent skiing in an alpine setting. Views from the various high points are unusual and stunning. The snowpack must be well frozen

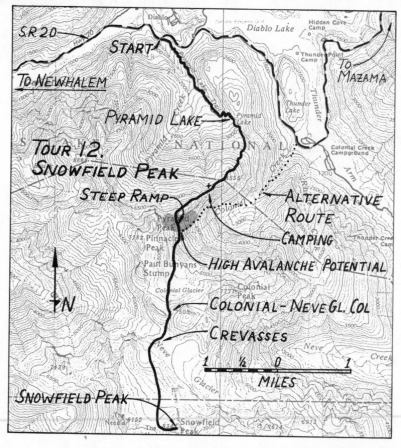

to make this tour safe. Skiers should watch for "glide cracks" in the snow below the Colonial Glacier, signs that the entire snow cover is creeping down the steep slabs and could fail catastrophically. Any tour into this area will be unusually brushy. Even if only part of the tour is done, you will get spectacular vistas and fine touring.

Drive State Route 20 east from Newhalem. Past Gorge Lake 0.5 mile is the Pyramid Lake trailhead. The trail leaves the road from the south side and climbs to Pyramid Lake (2600 feet) in 2.1 miles.

Pyramid Peak lies southwest of the lake. To get there climb south to the ridge descending northeast from the peak. It will be difficult to use skis below 4200 feet on the approach due to steep slopes, tight trees, and shallow snow cover. Snowshoes would be an aid here.

Good camping spots are found on a bench at 5400 feet, where the north face converges with the northeast ridge. Ski to the highest level of the bench (5800 feet), then peek over the edge to Colonial Creek basin (south). Descend a steep gully, then traverse steep slopes exposed to avalanches from Pyramid Peak. Climb a short 45- to 50-degree headwall to the northern edge of the Colonial Glacier, watching for glide cracks and thinly bridged streams on the headwall.

As you ascend the Colonial Glacier, the lay of the land becomes more apparent: You'll obtain a better view of Colonial Peak (on your left) and, from left to right, Paul Bunyans Stump, Pinnacle Peak, and Pyramid Peak will become clearly defined. You'll also see that Pyramid is really the northern terminus of the ridge crowned by the Stump and Pinnacle Peak. By this time you should be roped up: The Colonial Glacier is crevassed.

Continue climbing until you are on line between the Stump and Colonial Peak (about 6100 feet). Then ski due south for 0.5 mile to the gentle Colonial–Neve Glacier col (6840 feet) just west of the small, rocky hump (7505 feet) west of Colonial Peak.

There is something magic about reaching a pass in the high mountains. The gradual revealment of peaks and the sudden panorama is deeply thrilling. This pass, Snowfield Peak, and the Neve Glacier are exceptional.

From the gap, descend 300 feet to the broad saddle between the Neve and Ladder Creek glaciers (crevasses here). Continue south for 0.4 mile up the increasingly steep glacier. Pass the first steep section on the right, then ascend a southeast-trending ramp toward Snowfield Peak. The Neve Glacier is moderately crevassed but skiable.

Snowfield Peak is the highest peak in this subrange. The summit lies 1.6 ski miles from Col 6840, the leftmost peak. To reach Snowfield's summit, ski to the northwest ridge, then climb either the west ridge (class 3) or the north face.

Return by retracing the approach. A more direct descent (and ascent) involves descending the Colonial Creek drainage and escap-

The Neve Glacier is remote, high, and only moderately crevassed
(Photo: Harry Hendon).

ing near Thunder Arm. It is about 3.5 road miles from the Colonial
Creek trailhead to the Pyramid Lake trailhead.

This is a feasible route if there are at least two feet of snow at 2200
feet and the snowpack is well frozen. There are cliff bands near 3500
feet that can be passed on the steep north side of the valley. If there is
little snow, the brush near the valley bottom becomes a major obstacle. A faint trail can be found 300 feet or less east of Colonial Creek
below 1900 feet. Once you are below 3000 feet, descend the southeast
side of the creekbed to reach the bottom of the drainage. The brush
on this variation has been known to make grown men weep.

TEEBONE RIDGE

13

*Map —
page 64*

Start Point	Cascade River Road, 1200 feet
High Point	Little Devil Peak, 6985 feet
Best Time	December to May
Length	Weekend or long day trip; 8 miles; 9 hours
Difficulty	Advanced; high avalanche potential
Maps	Green Trails No. 47, Marblemount; USGS 15-minute series, Marblemount

This tour has year-round access in most years because the approach road, the Cascade River road, is below the snow line. It is probably more suitable in spring than in early season because of better snow cover and longer days.

This tour should only be attempted when the snowpack is well consolidated and air temperatures have been reasonably cool. The steep, grassy, south-facing slopes of Teebone Ridge provide an ideal environment for large avalanches. Ground avalanches are also a definite possibility in this area. Leave the area if it starts to rain or gets very hot.

One additional hazard is the occasional presence of bears. Observe recommended precautions in protecting your food. Park rangers will provide information on this.

Drive State Route 20 to Marblemount. Cross the Skagit River and continue east 7.5 miles on the Cascade River road to the Lookout Mountain–Monogram Lake trailhead. The trail climbs a rib on the steep hill on the north side of the road. If snow obscures the path, stay on the rib crest, or just right of it, for 2 miles (3000 feet). The lack of brush makes routefinding easy.

At 2 miles, the terrain begins to ease back and the prominent rib blends into the overall slope. Remain right of the west branch of Lookout Creek, heading roughly north and slightly west for 0.8 mile to a trail junction. The sign and trail may be covered with snow. In that case, at 2.8 miles (4200 feet) start making a right (northeast) traverse through an open forest of large fir and hemlock.

Continue skiing in a climbing traverse for 1 mile. The woods cease abruptly and a large, open basin, with a steepish crest on its right side appears. Take time to evaluate conditions. This basin is on the return route and avalanches frequently. Look up at the headwall: It is the western end of Teebone Ridge and it is possible, in good conditions, to ski directly down to the trail.

Be sure to note where you leave the woods so you can find your way back to the trail. Make a climbing traverse across the alp slope and ascend one of several gullies toward a slight pass on the crest (5400 feet).

Once at the crest, take a minute to look around at views of the surrounding peaks and Monogram Lake. The peak behind and left of the lake is a subsidiary summit (6840 feet) of Little Devil Peak (6985 feet). Little Devil is barely visible from this vantage point but the summits are less than 1 mile apart.

To avoid the long, exposed traverse below the crest of Teebone Ridge, descend to the right (southwest) shore of the lake, following a series of benches. Good, reasonably safe campsites may be made near the south shore.

To continue the ascent, cross Monogram Lake to its northeast shore and ascend a gentle gully to the pass north of a small knob (5607 feet). To continue, descend to benches beyond the pass and ascend up and right toward the moraine south of Haystack Glacier. Little Devil lies about 1.7 miles to the north. The glacier is gentle and presents no problems. Ski to its head and climb Little Devil by its southwest shoulder.

From the ridge you have great views of the Eldorado massif, Mount Baker, and Mount Shuksan. Also, a novel tour idea becomes apparent: Ski east over Little Devil and connect to Dorado Needle and Eldorado via Backbone Ridge. Then make your escape via Eldorado Creek, or Boston Basin, or. . . . This untested (but obvious) tour would be a bold route of distinctly alpine character.

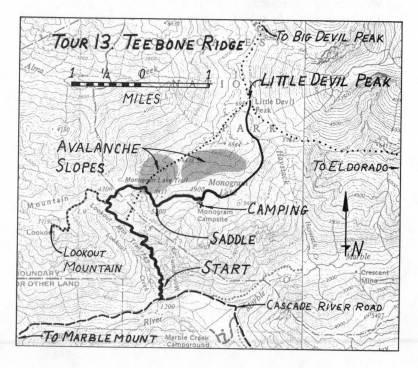

Aerial photo of Teebone Ridge looking north (Photo: Gary Brill).

Ski runs can be made partway down the Haystack Creek drainages (southeast) or back down to Monogram Lake. To return to the car, simply reverse the approach. A good alternative is to ski Teebone Ridge to its western end, then ski northwest toward your approach trail, descending the basin first seen when you left the forest. When you see where you left the woods, ski quickly out of the deposition zone and reenter the forest.

Allow enough time to get to your car in daylight since the last section of trail can be unpleasant in the dark. Small snowshoes can make the steep approach easier.

ELDORADO

14

Start Point	Cascade River Road, 2100 feet
High Point	Eldorado Peak, 8868 feet
Best Time	April to June
Length	Overnight; 12 miles; 11 hours
Difficulty	Advanced; glacier skiing; moderate avalanche potential
Maps	Green Trails Nos. 48 and 80, Diablo Dam and Cascade Pass; USGS 7.5-minute series, Eldorado Peak, Sonny Boy Lakes, Forbidden Peak, and Cascade Pass

Map — page 67

The Eldorado Tour provides rapid access to a remote area with many days of skiing. The approach via Eldorado Creek is straightforward. In early season most of the brush and talus is covered with snow, making both ascent and descent relatively pleasant. Go as soon as road conditions and weather allow, and take wax in addition to climbing skins.

Drive the Cascade River road east from Marblemount for nearly 20 miles. Park at the gravel pit on the right side of the road near the 20-mile marker and begin hiking north from the road. Cross the Cascade River on logs and climb north through open timber. Stay 100 to 200 feet left (west) of Eldorado Creek, which joins the river just upstream of your crossing. Be sure you are in the Eldorado rather than the Roush Creek drainage. Careful odometer observation should keep you from going wrong.

Climb for 1.5 miles, gaining about 1500 vertical feet. Climb to the right around an obvious buttress (about 4000 feet) and reach a talus field of house-sized blocks. Climbing over and around these huge boulders is exhausting but is obviated by an early-season tour. Continue heading due north for another 1.5 miles.

Just beyond the talus field (about 5000 feet), the angle eases off a

A deep, mid-season snowpack covers the boulder field above Eldorado Creek (Photo: Lowell Skoog, Brian Sullivan).

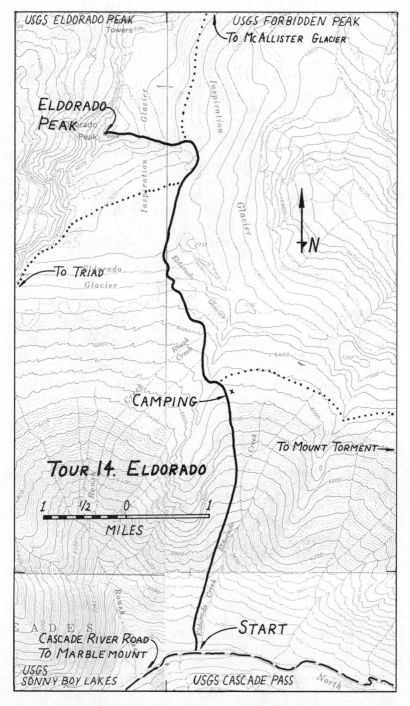

USGS ELDORADO PEAK
Towers

USGS FORBIDDEN PEAK
To McAllister Glacier

ELDORADO
PEAK
Eldorado
Peak

Inspiration Glacier

Glacier

N

To TRIAD

Eldorado
Glacier

Eldorado Glacier

Roush Creek

Creek

CAMPING

TOUR 14. ELDORADO

To MOUNT TORMENT

1   1/2   0   1
MILES

Eldorado Creek

START

C A S C A D E S

CASCADE RIVER ROAD
To MARBLEMOUNT

USGS
SONNY BOY LAKES

USGS CASCADE PASS

North

little, except for a few small cliff bands. Keep heading north (in late season, this section is an alder patch) until you reach gentler open slopes (meadows in summer). This area is a good place to make camp. From camp you can see the next obstacle: the crest dividing Eldorado and Roush creeks.

Head northwest for 0.3 mile and gain the ridge just above the 6000-foot level at a level section (about 500 feet below the looming cliffs).

From the rib descend 100 feet into the Roush Creek drainage and ski north and slightly west up the Eldorado Glacier, staying clear of the cliffs above your right. In 1 mile you should be abreast of Point 7733 (on your right) and on the Inspiration Glacier "flats." Rope up on the glacier and wand dubious crossings.

The route turns slightly east here, to make an end run around the east end of the south face of Eldorado (0.6 mile).

Once you reach the terminus of the south face, make a sharp left turn (head nearly due west) and ski or hike the last 0.8 mile (1400 feet) to the summit area. In most years the actual summit is a knife-edged snow arête, precipitous on either side. Mortals may require an ice ax and rope to climb to the true summit. Descend by retracing the approach.

A fine variation of this tour is to traverse east from the Eldorado high camp, crossing the rib south of Mount Torment at the 6650-foot notch to Boston Basin. There is a steep descent on the Boston side which sometimes requires a rappel. While you're looking around from the summit of Eldorado, notice the glacier northeast of the summit and consider the touring possibilities.

BOSTON BASIN

15

Map— page 70

Start Point	Cascade River Road, 3200 feet
High Point	Boston-Sahale Saddle, 6800 feet
Best Time	April to June
Length	Day trip; 8 miles; 6 hours
Difficulty	Intermediate; glacier skiing; high avalanche potential
Maps	Green Trails Nos. 48 and 80, Cascade Pass and Diablo Dam; USGS 7.5-minute series, Forbidden Peak and Cascade Pass

As spring turns to summer the Cascade River road melts out and gives access to the farther reaches of this mountain fastness. Boston Basin provides fine spring skiing and exciting views of Johannesberg's calving glaciers. The Boston Basin area suffers from overuse. Make only day trips to the basin, or pass on through to other more remote areas such as the McAllister Glacier. Do not enter Boston

Aerial photo of Boston Basin; compare photo with "topo" to locate Midas Creek (Photo: Gary Brill).

Basin when there is avalanche danger: Huge slides from the surrounding slopes *frequently* fill the entire area.

Drive the North Fork Cascade River road as far as conditions allow. There is a spur 5 miles (3200 feet) from Mineral Park. Park here. Hike the road northeast to the Diamond Mine and up the brushy hill above the building. The Diamond Mine is private property. Hikers and skiers may pass through the area but are asked not to interfere with the property.

The unofficial trail is muddy, brushy, and steep, and it leaves the cleared area near its left upper side. Continue hiking uphill through forest, sometimes following streambeds.

Timberline is near 5000 feet and the terrain becomes more level. Midas Creek is the stream on your left as you leave the woods. Make note of landmarks to be able to find the way back.

Ski out of the sheltering trees and climb the large moraine ahead. From this vantage you can see the route to the Boston–Sahale saddle. Ski ahead to 6300 feet, then traverse northeast, staying well clear (left) of the cliffs at the foot of Sahale Peak. In 1000 feet you are on glacier and skiing toward Sharkfin Tower. When convenient, simply head directly toward the broad saddle. The Boston Glacier is crevassed.

Another good objective is the col on the north ridge of Mount Torment near 6650 feet. This is a half-day tour.

On descending, make certain you find the right entrance to the woods above Midas Creek. Taking the wrong drainage would result in a long, unpleasant, and dangerous bushwhack out.

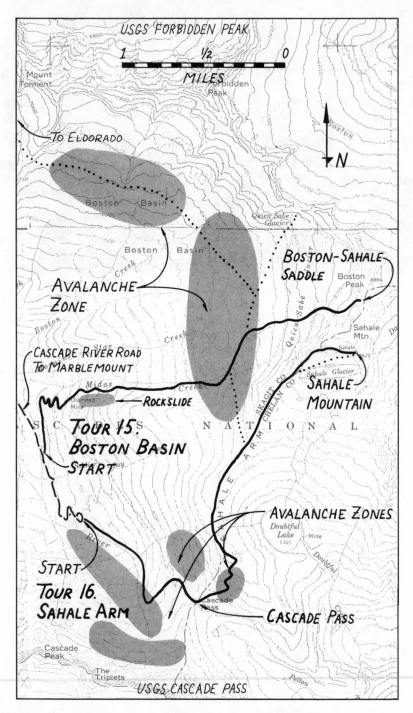

SAHALE ARM

16

Start Point	Cascade River Road End, 3600 feet
High Point	Sahale Mountain, 8715 feet
Best Time	March to June
Length	Day trip; 6 miles; 7 hours
Difficulty	Advanced; glacier travel for summit climb; high avalanche potential
Maps	Green Trails Nos. 48 and 80, Cascade Pass and Diablo Dam; USGS 7.5-minute series, Forbidden Peak and Cascade Pass

Cascade Pass is one of the most spectacular, easily accessible viewpoints in the North Cascades. It is also the entry point for at

Descending Sahale Arm (Photo: Gary Brill).

least two important high routes, the Ptarmigan Traverse and the Boston Basin–Eldorado high route. The skiing is pretty good in the immediate vicinity of the pass, too.

Drive the Cascade River road as far as conditions permit. Road end comes in 25 long miles at 3600 feet. Leave the road from the right shoulder at the curve just below the parking loop and head straight up (southeast) the drainage toward Cascade Pass. Some routefinding is needed to penetrate the short cliff bands that break up the snow slope. Nevertheless, the direct ascent is desirable in early season because it is short (1.5 miles) and avoids avalanche slopes below Sahale Arm. However, remember that very large avalanches can descend from Cascade Pass and The Triplets, filling the entire basin. Well settled snow is required for this tour.

From Cascade Pass climb east of the narrow crest leading to Sahale Arm. This area is steep, south facing, and frequently releases wet-snow avalanches, even in early summer. In 0.5 mile and 800 feet, you reach the east shoulder of the Arm and obtain views of Doubtful Lake to the north. Follow the ridge northwest past Point 6263, then continue north toward Sahale itself. Follow the western margin of the glacier to the summit slabs, then scramble to the summit.

Descend by retracing the approach down to Cascade Pass. Cliff bands below Sahale Arm and avalanche gullies on the north face of the Triplets make the descent problematic. From the pass, descend 0.2 mile to the northwest, to 5000 feet. Head southwest for 0.1 mile, dropping 200 feet. Descend a very steep section for another 200 feet, avoiding cliffs to the west, then ski the fall line to the parking lot. This is a fine, but dangerous run.

This tour is best made as soon as road conditions permit access. Leave the area if rain starts to threaten. Start early in the day to minimize the danger from wet-snow avalanches and be meticulous in evaluating conditions before setting out.

SNOWKING MOUNTAIN

17

Start Point	Illabot Creek Road, 2946 feet
High Point	Snowking Mountain, 7433 feet
Best Time	April to June
Length	Day trip; 16 miles; 12 hours
Difficulty	Advanced; glacier travel; navigation; high avalanche potential
Maps	Green Trails No. 79, Snowking Mountain; USGS 7.5-minute series, Snowking Mountain

Snowking Mountain and its companion, Mount Buckindy, are not usually seen by roadbound travelers. This area is fairly unknown

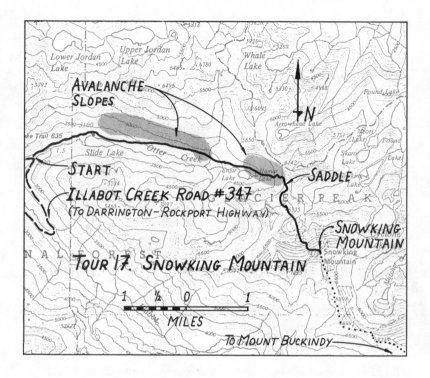

even to many mountain skiers. Nevertheless, Snowking is a good spring tour with reasonable accessibility. The Illabot Creek road puts the skier into the area with less than 5 miles of walking (or skiing).

Drive State Route 20 to Rockport. Take the Rockport-Darrington road south, crossing the Skagit River almost immediately. (Take a moment to appreciate the view of the Eldorado massif from the bridge.) South of Rockport 2.5 miles is the Illabot Creek road. Stay on this main road for 10 miles. It begins to switchback up a hill. In 1 mile the road divides. Take the left fork and begin heading north. Contour clockwise around the Illabot Peaks. Soon you are heading east, then southeast up the Illabot drainage. Keep to the main road, avoiding spurs. You will cross Iron, Bluebell, and Arrow creeks before you reach Illabot Creek. Drive the last 2 miles to Otter Creek (2945 feet) and park the car 22 miles from the highway.

Begin hiking on the Slide Lake trail (No. 635). The trail heads east. If there is adequate snow cover, you can follow Otter Creek cross country, keeping about 200 yards north of the stream. The lake is reached in 1.5 miles (there is a trail in summer).

Continue skiing past Slide Lake (3110 feet), making an eastward

Mutchler Peak from Snowking Mountain; touring extraordinaire (Photo: Brian Sullivan).

climbing traverse for 2.6 miles along open and some wooded slopes. Enjar and Hamar lakes are nestled in the basin (4300 feet) at the head of the valley (3 miles from Slide Lake). Circle these on the left and make a climbing traverse to the saddle (east of the lakes, about 5100 feet). The summit of Snowking lies 1.4 miles south of the saddle.

Make a southeast traverse along the north-trending shoulder to reach the summit (7433 feet). From the summit plateau, skiers have a number of options. Side trips can be made in any direction: west; east along the Snowking and the Mutchler glaciers; south toward Illabot Creek; or north. To return to the car, simply retrace your approach route.

Or, skiers can descend to Illabot Creek, heading due west until they cross the access road (4.6 miles).

This tour is exposed to avalanche danger near Enjar Lake and on the alternative descent route. Since it is a spring tour when the snowpack is fairly consolidated, avalanches should not be a problem unless it is very hot or raining. Skiers can connect ridges to nearby peaks such as Mount Buckindy and Mount Chaval. To do so, requires an overnight stay and good weather.

ANDERSON BUTTE

18

Start Point	Anderson Lakes Trail, 4300 feet
High Point	Anderson Butte, 5700 feet; or Mount Watson, 6234 feet
Best Time	May to June
Length	Day trip; 7 miles; 6 hours
Difficulty	Advanced; glacier skiing on Mount Watson; moderate avalanche potential
Maps	Green Trails No. 46, Lake Shannon; USGS 15-minute series, Lake Shannon

*Map—
page 76*

Close views of Mount Shuksan and Bacon Peak are some of the delights of this tour. Anderson Butte and Mount Watson lie between Baker Lake and Bacon Peak and are easily accessible in a day tour.

Drive State Route 20 to Birdsview, 21 miles east of Interstate 5. Turn north on the Baker Lake road (No. 25), driving to the upper Baker Dam (13 miles). Cross the dam (road No. 1106) and head east, then north to the trailhead (road No. 1107, 10 miles, 4300 feet). Note: If you find yourself heading south along Baker Lake, you've taken the wrong turnoff. Do not leave valuables in your vehicle.

The road is snow covered in early season and may be difficult to descend when icy. Ski to the trailhead and continue 2 miles to a fork. To reach Anderson Butte, take the left fork to the Anderson Butte summit ridge (0.8 mile, 5400 feet). The true summit is on the eastern end of the ridge (5700 feet). Make sure snow conditions are stable before venturing onto open slopes. There are excellent views from the summit and good ski runs to the northwest.

To descend from the summit ridge, make a 1000-foot run to the north, then traverse west for 0.7 mile until you can turn the corner (northwest shoulder of Anderson Butte) on your left. Once past the corner, head slightly southwest and descend until you cross the approach road (about 1.2 miles). Alternatively, you can continue the counterclockwise tour, traversing near 4600 feet until you rejoin the trail and re-ascend to the fork.

To reach Mount Watson, take the middle fork and climb to Watson Lakes. Anderson Lakes, reached via the right fork, are *not* the objective. (If you lose the trail, remember that Watson Lakes [there are two] are located east of the trailhead and north of Mount Watson.) Climb 0.3 mile to a small saddle (5000 feet). Traverse east for 1 mile, descending slightly, then climb southeast to a saddle between the two summits of Mount Watson. This part of the tour takes place on a small glacier. The saddle is a good place for lunch, and a good turnaround spot since the summits require class 3 climbing.

Runs are possible most frequently on the northern flank of Mount Watson. In some seasons it is possible to traverse east to a small glacier and snowfield on the eastern flank of the peak. If not, de-

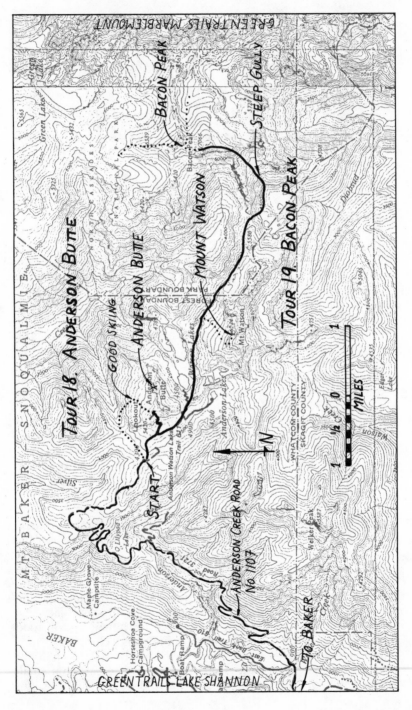

scend the main glacier and traverse around the bottom (north) side to ascend this ice body. Retrace the approach to return to the car.

This tour provides a pleasant approach to Bacon Peak. Simply continue traversing below the Watson glaciers toward Bacon Peak (see Tour 19).

BACON PEAK

19

Start Point	Anderson Lakes Trailhead, 4300 feet; or Baker Lake Road, 820 feet
High Point	Bacon Peak, 7070 feet
Best Time	May to July
Length	17 miles; 2 to 3 days
Difficulty	Advanced; navigation; glacier skiing; high avalanche potential
Maps	Green Trails No. 46, Lake Shannon; USGS 15-minute series, Lake Shannon

Bacon Peak, a massive plateau east of Baker Lake, is unknown to many mountaineers: It is invisible from State Route 20 and hard to approach from any side. Nevertheless, its large glaciers and snowfields and its remote situation offer the possibility of a real adventure within hours of the Puget Sound region.

A good late-season approach is made via the Anderson Lakes trail, No. 611, described in Tour 18.

Hike the trail to the first fork, at 2 miles, then take the middle fork to Watson Lakes. The lakes are reached in 1.5 miles from the fork.

From the lakes traverse east above their south shores. The northern slopes of Mount Watson are steep, open, and prone to avalanche; they should only be crossed when the snowpack is well frozen. Continue for 2 miles, passing below the buttress on your right. The snout of a lesser glacier will appear above you. Continue traversing southeast, then east, to the saddle dividing Diobsud and Noisy Creek drainages (4900 feet, another mile).

The route heads southeast into a basin. Pause to consider slope stability before leaving the saddle. Once in the basin, climb left (northeast) to Diobsud Glacier and to the summit plateau. The route to the summit, a northeast trek, is self-evident. Descend via the approach.

An alternative route, with a bad reputation for low-level brush, involves climbing the Noisy Creek drainage. Drive the Baker Lake road to its terminus (28 miles), past Baker Lake to the Baker River valley (800 feet, road No. 1168).

From road's end, hike southeast to the river and ford where possible. After the crossing turn right and follow an incipient trail

Mounts Hagan and Bacon in the middle distance, looking south (Photo: Brian Sullivan).

southwest along Baker Lake. Alternatively, you could rent a boat at Tarr's Resort (22.4 miles on the Baker Lake road) to avoid the river crossing.

Hike for 2.5 miles and turn left up the Noisy Creek drainage. Follow the way path on the east side of the stream through dense forest, crossing the creek in 1 mile.

Continue upstream (south) for 2 miles until you reach Heather Creek (2300 feet). This stream descends from Green Lake, which lies in a pocket (4300 feet) 3 miles east of Noisy Creek.

Climb this drainage, keeping left (north) of the stream. There is a way path, often overgrown. The valley begins to level near 4700 feet and offers good campsites (8 hours from the trailhead). There are cliff bands with waterfalls above camp. Pass these on the left and climb 400 feet to a pass. Green Lake is below and east of you.

From the saddle, Bacon Peak summit is 2.2 miles away to the south. Begin the approach by heading slightly east, then crossing a small glacier. Enter a steep trough leading to the Green Lake Glacier and make a right-heading (south) traverse toward the summit (7070 feet).

Once on the plateau you have numerous touring options: Ski the Green Lake, the Noisy Creek (northwest), or Diobsud (southeast) glaciers. A fine high route involves skiing north to Mount Hagan or even Mount Blum. Descend by retracing the route of ascent.

MOUNT SHUKSAN

20

Start Point	Shannon Creek Road, 2500 feet	
High Point	Mount Shuksan, 9127 feet	
Best Time	February to June	
Length	Day trip; 12 miles; 9 hours	
Difficulty	Advanced; glacier travel; moderate avalanche potential	
Maps	Green Trails Nos. 14 and 46, Mount Shuksan and Lake Shannon; USGS 15-minute series, Mount Shuksan and Lake Shannon	

*Map—
page 81*

The Mount Shuksan Tour has, for some skiers, an aspect of pilgrimage. Barely visible from most lowland vantage points (it is visible from high places in Seattle), the mountain only reveals itself as you approach it more closely. Once on its icy south flank, you'll wonder how you ever got there, and how you'll get back.

Although this is not a technically difficult tour, it does hold some avalanche hazard, especially on the lower portions of the Sulphide Glacier. Be meticulous in your hazard evaluation before committing to slopes that are exposed to hazard.

Drive the Baker Lake road past Koma Kulshan guard station and Baker Lake Campground. Past the campground 5 miles (well before Shannon Creek), turn left on the Shuksan Lake road (No. 1152, signed). In 0.2 mile turn right to the first fork and drive for 3 miles to a junction. Take the right fork and follow it north into the Shannon Creek drainage to a washout, about 1.5 miles.

Hike or ski the road for about 1 mile, until you round a corner and are confronted by a clearcut. You may ski the road or ascend the

On the Sulphide Glacier (Photo: Gary Brill).

clearcut, heading north into the woods. The objective is the right side of the obvious ridge above you.

Continue skiing through open woods for 1 mile, breaking out of the timber near 4800 feet. A small notch lies to the northeast, your gateway to the Sulphide Glacier. The slopes facing you are known to slide. Check it out. In case of instability, abandon the tour and ski small bowls on lower ridges. Note that afternoon sun can warm this slope and create wet-snow sluffs. Time your descents so as to escape this last hazard on your way out.

Climb to the notch (about 5400 feet, USGS map is in error) and look around at the views. Look, too, at your route. Just north of your perch is Point 6466. Your first task is to descend from the notch, bypassing the cornices on the east side. Caution: The eastern slope of this saddle and the adjacent steep south slope often develop wind-slab. If you suspect windslab, abandon the tour. Watch also for icy conditions on the traverse beyond the notch.

Next, you must traverse around the steep, 35-degree slope beneath Point 6466 for about 600 feet to get to easier ground. Cliffs and a deep gully below increase the need for caution here.

If you camp above the notch, *any* significant snowfall may create serious avalanche hazard here and prevent your return to the notch.

Once you gain the small crest at the east end of the traverse, begin heading north to the snout of the Sulphide. Stay to the left, fairly close (but not too close, cornices and avalanches) to the cliffs on your left to avoid cliffs and crevasses. Consider wanding the route from here on since a whiteout will make the descent problematic. The lower part of the glacier is quite flat but steepens above 6500 feet. The glacier becomes increasingly broken up toward the east.

Continue skiing upslope, generally keeping to the left to avoid crevasses, to the summit pyramid, which may be climbed via gullies in its southwest face. These gullies slide frequently, especially in the afternoon sun. Many skiers feel content to rest after the ascent, knowing that there is a 3000-foot run awaiting them.

The adventurous can cross the southeast ridge of the summit pyramid near 8100 feet and ski 1.3 miles north across the Crystal Glacier toward the north shoulder of Mount Shuksan. This side trip puts the skier above the Nooksack Glacier and, if glacier conditions allow you to approach the edge, gives unusual views of Nooksack Tower. Ropes are essential since crevasses abound and run in many directions. This trip takes about 3 hours.

A wonderful variation requiring an overnight stay is a circum-navigation of the summit pyramid. This side trip involves only moderate skiing in a very scenic alpine setting.

Back on the Sulphide, the descent looks improbable. Cliffs plunge to unseen canyons on all sides, and the way down is not obvious. Begin by following your tracks. Stay reasonably close to the western (right) edge of the Sulphide Glacier during the descent. Do not ski the fall line (southeast) toward Sulphide Lake. The eastern edge of the Sulphide and the lower Crystal Glacier are extremely broken up. Do not descend through the notch at 6380 feet, just above the first pinnacle visible from the pass. This descent route looks good but leads to very steep slopes below. The notch at 5400 feet used in the ascent is the only reasonable return route. Wands placed on the ascent help in finding it if the weather turns bad.

Before making the descending traverse to the notch, evaluate conditions once again. It is better to wait until the slopes stabilize, even if it means a bivouac, than to risk a ride over the cliffs below. Once over the pass, pause again to pick a safe route, through the open west-facing slopes, back to your car.

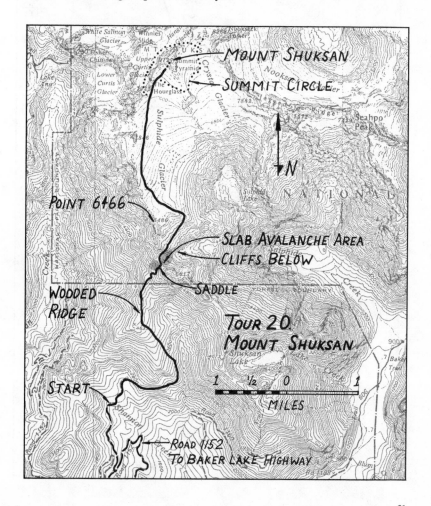

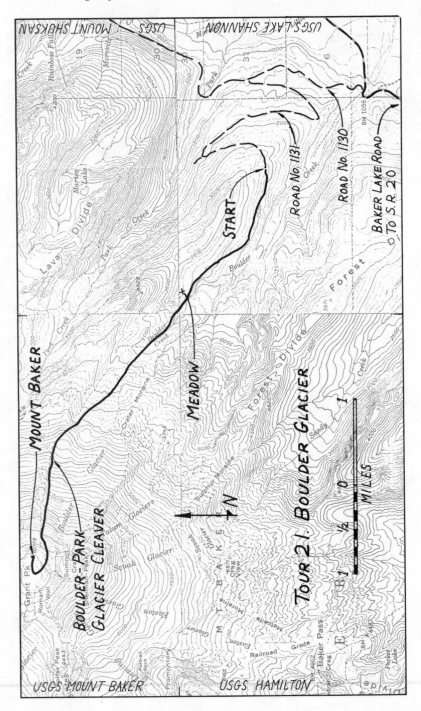

MOUNT BAKER: BOULDER GLACIER

21

Start Point	Boulder Creek Trailhead, 2700 feet
High Point	Mount Baker Summit, 10,778 feet
Best Time	May to July
Length	Overnight; 8 miles; 13 hours to summit
Difficulty	Advanced; glacier travel; moderate avalanche potential; lahar warning
Maps	Green Trails Nos. 13, 14, and 45, Mount Baker, Mount Shuksan, and Hamilton; USGS 15-minute series, Mount Shuksan, Mount Baker, and Lake Shannon

Boulder Glacier is not only a popular climbing route, it is also an excellent mid- to late-season ski tour due to the easy approach and good spring skiing. Geothermal activity near Sherman Crater has resulted in lahar (snow and earth slide) warnings on the route. Avoid it if there are signs of thermal activity.

Drive the Baker Lake road for 17 miles and turn left on the Crater Moraine road. In 1.7 miles there is a fork. Turn left up a hairpin turn (road No. 1131) and switchback up Crater Moraine to the trailhead (2600 feet, 2.5 miles).

Below Park and Boulder glaciers (Photo: Brian Sullivan).

Hike or ski a road remnant heading northwest through an old clearcut. In 0.2 miles you'll reach old-growth forest. Continue skiing through the woods, passing a small meadow (3400 feet, 2.1 miles). Continue skiing northwest (way path in summer) in a climbing traverse along the south side of Crater Moraine. Watch for sluffs from the steep slopes above here.

In 0.5 mile you'll come to a shallow gully. Ascend this groove to the crest of Boulder Ridge. Timberline here is at 5000 feet. There are good campsites here among trees. Above camp lies Crater Moraine. Head northwest, keeping right of a ravine bearing northwest. Continue skiing northwest on the moraine to bypass the snout of Boulder Glacier on its right flank (6000 feet). The crevassed section of the lower Boulder Glacier is bypassed on the right by keeping to the crest of Crater Moraine. Continue climbing west to the base of Boulder-Park Glacier cleaver, ascending this rib directly to avoid crevasses on either side. Make a left-climbing traverse near 10,000 feet to avoid cliffs, and climb to the summit area. Do not attempt the steep summit climb under icy conditions unless your party is properly equipped.

Descend the route of ascent. In most seasons, the skiing is best below 9000 feet.

MOUNT BAKER: EASTON GLACIER

22

Start Point	Schreibers Meadow Trailhead, 3200 feet	
High Point	Mount Baker Summit, 10,778 feet	
Best Time	April to July	
Length	Long day or overnight; 11 miles; 10 hours	
Difficulty	Advanced; glacier travel; moderate avalanche potential	
Maps	Green Trails Nos. 13 and 45, Mount Baker and Hamilton; USGS 15-minute series, Mount Baker and Hamilton	

Ever expanding vistas, with the spectacular Black Buttes as nearby companions, describe this tour in good weather. While most mortals will require a two-day trip to reach the summit, even skiing to 7000 or 8000 feet will give skiers a long run with grand views and varied terrain.

Drive east on State Route 20 from Sedro Wooley for 14.4 miles and turn left on the Baker Lake road. Drive this road for 12.5 miles, then turn left on the Loomis–Nooksack road No. 12. Continue for 3.5 miles to the junction of the Loomis–Nooksack and Schreibers Meadow roads. Turn right and drive for 0.5 mile, keeping left at the Dillard Point road. Drive another 1.5 miles and keep left at the next fork. Drive 3 to 5 miles up the road to where the snow blocks your way.

Signs indicate the trailhead to Schreibers Meadow and Sulphur Creek. Follow orange markers to Schreibers Meadow (0.5 mile).

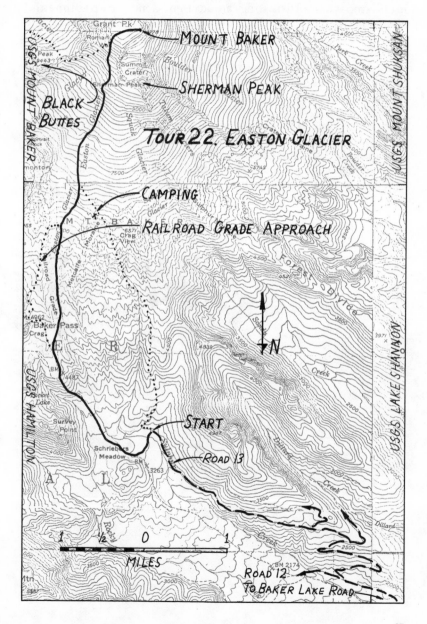

Once through the meadow, you can turn right (north) at the streambed and ski directly up the former bed of the Easton Glacier toward the summit of Mount Baker. Stay well clear of sluffs that might descend from the moraines to either side. Once you climb out of the trough left by the receding glacier, you are skiing on the glacier itself—ropes and prusik slings are advised. Continue up as time and energy allow, passing to the left of Sherman Peak and its crater. The crater notch is at 9700 feet. To reach the summit, stay just left of the cliffs above the crater notch.

Be sure to allow enough time for the descent. In early season, the lower slopes freeze hard as soon as they fall into the shadow of the Railroad Grade moraine. The resulting conditions can only be called gruesome.

Another route to the Easton Glacier is to head north from the road end, climbing through clearcuts and timber. Cross shallow gullies on a moraine to reach good camp spots near 5500 feet. Ski north along a ridge to reach the glacier. This approach avoids early-season snowmobilers at Schreibers Meadow.

On the edge of Sherman Crater (Photo: Harry Hendon).

MOROVITZ MEADOWS

23

Start Point	Schreibers Meadow Trailhead, 3200 feet
High Point	Morovitz Meadows, 4500 feet; or Park Butte, 5450 feet
Best Time	April to June
Length	Day trip; 8 miles; 7 hours
Difficulty	Intermediate; moderate avalanche potential
Maps	Green Trails Nos. 45 and 46, Hamilton and Lake Shannon; USGS 15-minute series, Lake Shannon and Hamilton

Morovitz Meadows and adjacent slopes offer lots of skiing, ranging from novice hills to very advanced runs. The summit of nearby Park Butte is a good place for viewing Twin Sisters and Mount Baker too. As the snowpack diminishes late in spring, the approach becomes more manageable and snowmobiles are excluded (by USFS

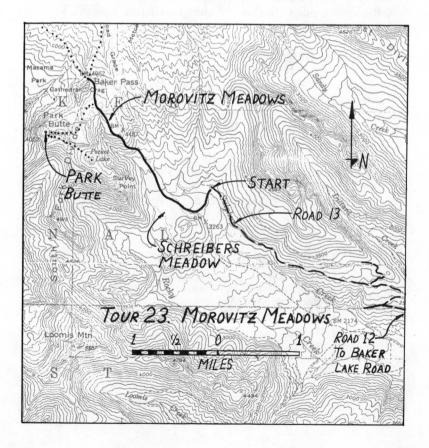

regulation) from Schreibers Meadow. The result is a pleasant tour in spring conditions.

Drive to the Schreibers Meadow trailhead (see Tour 22). Cross Sulphur Creek, following orange metal markers, and ski northwest to Schreibers Meadow (3263 feet, 0.5 mile). Continue northwest for another mile, crossing the stream descending from the Easton Glacier. Continue into the woods, climbing the steep summer trail to lower Morovitz Meadows (1 mile, 4100 feet). Beware of avalanche tracks that cross some of the switchbacks.

Upper Morovitz Meadows (4500 feet) is just to the north. There is a trail junction here (buried under snow, most likely) the left fork leading to Park Butte and the right leading to Baker Pass, Mazama Park, and the Railroad Grade, the giant moraine left by a receding Easton Glacier. Ski west from the upper meadow, traversing below the south slope of Cathedral Crag. Climb the eastern slope of Park Butte to reach the summit (5450 feet, 1 mile).

Views from the summit area are spectacular and afford a close look into the snowy side of the Twin Sisters Range (see Tour 24). Look to see if you can find other likely tours.

The best runs descend the eastern flank of Park Butte. The west side is cliffy. From the summit, skiers can traverse the ridge to the southeast to reach Survey Point (5100 feet, 1 mile) or descend to Pocket Lake, or both. A direct descent from Pocket Lake to Schreibers Meadow is possible, but steep in places. Survey Point is very steep on its eastern flanks. It's more feasible to make a northwest descending traverse to Pocket Lake, then descend east to the upper north fork of Rocky Creek. From there it's a short run to Schreibers Meadow and to the car. The final miles are made more pleasant if you have wax instead of climbing skins (or nonwaxing skis).

Alternatively, you may descend the route of ascent and visit the Mazama Park area 1.5 miles west of Baker Pass.

TWIN SISTERS

24		
	Start Point	Dailey Prairie Road, 3000 feet
	High Point	Twin Sisters Saddle, 5850 feet
	Best Time	April to June
	Length	Day trip; 7 miles; 5 hours
	Difficulty	Intermediate; glacier travel; moderate avalanche potential
	Maps	Green Trails No. 45, Hamilton; USGS 15-minute series, Wickersham

The run down the north side of Twin Sisters Saddle offers nearly 2000 feet of prime skiing as late as June. In addition, this skiing takes

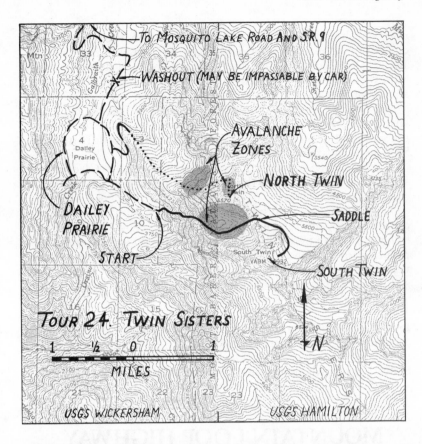

Map labels: To Mosquito Lake Road And S.R. 9 · Washout (May Be Impassable By Car) · Avalanche Zones · North Twin · Saddle · Dailey Prairie · Start · South Twin · Tour 24 Twin Sisters · Miles · N · USGS Wickersham · USGS Hamilton

place in a scenic, uncrowded environment that's relatively close to Pugetopolis. The area surrounding the Twin Sisters Range has been clearcut, but the logging roads provide the access to this area. Georgia-Pacific Corporation (Timber Department, at Clearview) can give you information about road conditions if you call (206) 733-4410 during business hours.

Drive State Route 9 to the town of Acme. If you are coming from the north, turn left on the Mosquito Lake road just before the town (immediately north of the Nooksack River bridge). If you are coming from the south, drive past Acme and turn right on the Mosquito Lake road. Drive this road 7.5 miles to the Nooksack Middle Fork bridge and 0.5 mile beyond to join road No. 38.

Turn right on road No. 38 and drive it for 4 miles (headlights on for safety).

Cross a curved concrete bridge and in 0.3 mile turn right onto (down) the first road (may be gated). At 0.4 mile cross the Middle Fork Nooksack River and drive for about 4 miles to a junction. By now, you should have a pretty good idea of where the range is. Your objective is to reach the valley between the two west ridges of the Twin Sisters. Drive in that direction until you can drive no more. More detail becomes irrelevant due to washouts, logging operations, and other obstacles.

Ski directly (east) to the valley between the two peaks. If you suspect avalanche activity, abandon the tour. Otherwise continue up the valley until a col becomes visible to the right of North Twin (about 5900 feet). Head directly for the col.

Make a short eastbound descent to cross the Sisters Glacier, then ski the firn as far down as the snow (and slope) permits. There are cliffs below 4400 feet.

A good side trip is to traverse right (south) from the saddle you came through, around the graceful north ridge of South Twin, and to the north face of South Twin. This face is a good snow climb in the proper, early-season conditions. There is often a large bergschrund near 6200 feet in mid- to late season. Return to the Twin Sisters saddle via the approach route. Ropes are strongly suggested for skiing the glacier as it is well crevassed.

Return to the car by descending from the saddle. Do not make this tour in very hot weather since the western valley may become an avalanche trap in the late afternoon.

An alternative tour skirts the north side of the north peak of Twin Sisters. Two bowls offer good skiing and a change of scenery.

MOUNTAIN LOOP HIGHWAY AND STATE ROUTE 530

The tours in this region have a wild flavor. The western tours are wild because of their gloomy and precipitous aspect, and the eastern tours are so because of their remoteness.

The main rivers of the area are the Sauk, the Suiattle, and the White Chuck. Most roads follow these drainages, enabling mountain travelers to reach areas ranging from Whitehorse Mountain in the west to Dome Peak in the northeast. The tours in this area are good in early or late season. Midwinter access is usually difficult, except to Whitehorse Mountain.

Mount Pilchuck is included in this section because of its proximity to Darrington. This western outpost of the North-Central Cascades is accessible from the Mountain Loop Highway.

Current information about road and snow conditions can sometimes be obtained at the USFS ranger station east of Darrington on the Darrington-Rockport highway.

GLACIER PEAK

25

Start Point	White Chuck River Trailhead, 2300 feet
High Point	Glacier Peak, 10,541 feet
Best Time	May to June
Length	Overnight; 24 miles; 14 hours
Difficulty	Advanced; glacier travel; moderate avalanche potential
Maps	Green Trails Nos. 111 and 112, Sloan Peak and Glacier Peak; USGS 15-minute series, Glacier Peak

Map— page 92

A spring ski ascent of Glacier Peak, although properly in a wilderness area, can hardly be thought of as a "wilderness experience." The number of persons entering this area increases every year. One recent Fourth of July saw over 40 skiers on the summit of the volcano. Such crowds may make it difficult to find campsites in Boulder Basin. Come early, or avoid high-use periods such as holidays. Take a rope, ice axes, and crampons.

Glacier Peak in late summer conditions (Photo: Tad Pfeffer).

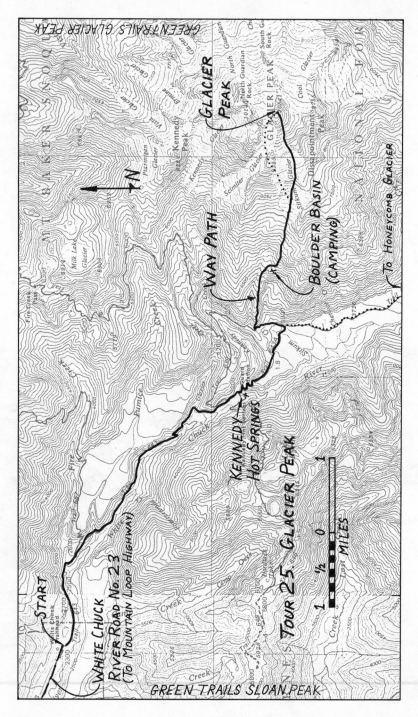

Drive State Route 530 to Darrington. Head south from Darrington on the Mountain Loop Highway. Drive 10.5 miles past the Sauk River bridge and turn left on the White Chuck River road (No. 23). Drive 10.5 miles to the road's end (2300 feet), or as far as snow permits.

Hike the undulating White Chuck River trail past Kennedy Hot Springs (5.3 miles, 3300 feet) to its junction with the Cascade Crest Trail (7.1 miles, 3900 feet). Turn left at the junction and hike north for 0.5 mile. Look for a way path descending from the steep hill on your right.

The route follows this wooded ridge near its crest. In early season the path may be obscured by snow. In that case, climb the ridge for 1.5 miles to timberline (5600 feet). Head due east until you begin to clear the trees, then turn south (right) slightly to enter Boulder Basin. This basin is a good place to camp, especially the heather bench across the stream. Pitch your tent well out of the way of snow slides that may occur.

Continue to climb southeast toward the crest above the basin, keeping right of the headwall above and to your left. Gain the crest (7600 feet) and turn left, heading uphill in a northeastern direction. There are two approaches to the summit. The one most suitable for skiers climbs due east, surmounting a few glacier rolls to reach the final couloir. This broad, moderately steep gully leads directly to the summit area and is also the best descent route. The other final approach crosses the saddle below the west summit ridge. Contour around left over steep, exposed slopes until you can climb a large chute to the summit area.

To return to camp, simply ski down the southwest summit slope and follow your tracks down to Boulder Basin.

One of the highlights of this tour is the opportunity to soak in Kennedy Hotsprings on the hike out. Please don't use soap in the hot spring or near the river.

HONEYCOMB AND SUIATTLE GLACIERS

26

Start Point	White Chuck River Trailhead, 2300 feet
High Point	White River-Suiattle Divide, 8100 feet
Best Time	May to July
Length	4 days; 28 miles; 22 hours
Difficulty	Advanced; glacier travel; moderate avalanche potential
Maps	Green Trails Nos. 111 and 112, Sloan Peak and Glacier Peak; USGS 15-minute series, Sloan Peak and Glacier Peak

Map— page 95

This tour is long but is considered by many to be the best wilderness tour in the Glacier Peak area. The Suiattle and Honeycomb

Spring corn on the Suiattle Glacier (Photo: Gary Brill).

glaciers are visible from Nason Ridge and other high vantage points near U.S. 2. These glaciers (and a third, the White Chuck) are the "big snowfields" to the left and south of Glacier Peak, as seen from Jim Hill Mountain. Because of the long approach, lightweight equipment is recommended for this tour.

Hike the White Chuck River trail (see Tour 25) to Kennedy Hot Springs and camp. Enjoy a warm, bubbling soak in the hot springs (if you can find room). Very hardy people may continue on to the Crest Trail and then to Glacier Peak Meadows (12 miles from the road, 5400 feet). This trail contours above the White Chuck River, crossing it 9.5 miles from the trailhead. The trail begins to head west near the

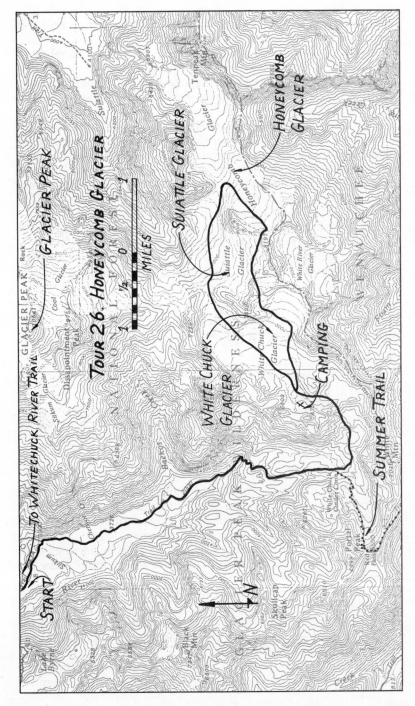

5500-foot level, due east of White Chuck Cinder Cone. Leave the trail here: Turn left and head east toward a broad ramp.

This hill is bounded by cliffs on either side. Ascend it straight on to gain the plateau and the glaciers above (1.5 miles, 900 feet to plateau). Once you reach the plateau, look for two small peaks 0.5 mile to your left (north). There are tarns just east of these pinnacles, a good spot for high camp. Make camp and begin exploring.

From camp, head due east to the 0.5-mile-wide eastern lobe of the White Chuck Glacier. Ski to its head, then descend east over a saddle to the Suiattle Glacier. From here you can traverse all over the Honeycomb and Suiattle glaciers, and Glacier Peak as well. This area deserves an entire week of attention. To return to high camp you may make a circle around point 7829, then descend the White Chuck to your tent. Reverse the approach to return to the car.

A noteworthy high route can be made by descending Red Pass to the White River drainage and skiing out toward the east.

A spectacular high route here is a traverse of the Dakobed Range, starting from the White Chuck River and exiting over Clark Mountain.

MEADOW MOUNTAIN

27		
	Start Point	Crystal Creek Road, 3000 feet
	High Point	Meadow Mountain Summit, 6324 feet
	Best Time	November; April to May
	Length	Day trip; 7 miles; 6 hours
	Difficulty	Intermediate; moderate avalanche potential
	Maps	Green Trails Nos. 111 and 112, Sloan Peak and Glacier Peak; USGS 7.5-minute series, Glacier Peak 3 N.E.

This short tour is distinguished more for its easy access and reasonable early-season skiing than its spectacular runs; nevertheless, the upper meadows offer pleasant 600-foot runs and fine views of nearby peaks.

Drive south on the Mountain Loop Highway from Darrington for 10.5 miles. Just south of the White Chuck River bridge leave the highway and drive east on the White Chuck River road for 6.1 miles. Turn north onto the Straight Creek road and follow it through switchbacks into the Crystal Creek drainage. In 2.4 miles, the Meadow Mountain road (No. 2710) forks east. This spur traverses the south slope of Meadow Mountain but is blocked by a slide 0.2 mile from the fork (may be gated).

From the car (about 3000 feet), ski or hike northeast 1.5 miles to the ridge crest (5200 feet), then meander along the crest to the summit of

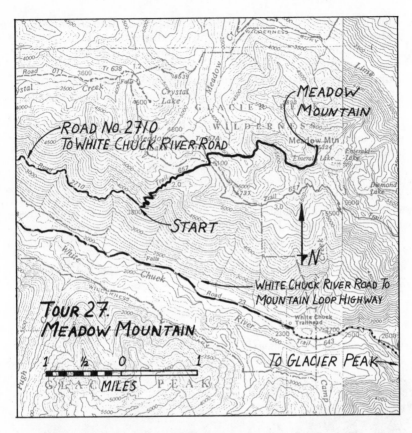

Meadow Mountain. Numerous runs can be made in the open meadows below. Allow enough time to return to the car by dark.

GREEN MOUNTAIN

28

Start Point	Green Mountain Road, 3800 feet
High Point	Green Mountain, 6500 feet
Best Time	November to May
Length	Day trip; 8 miles; 6 hours
Difficulty	Advanced; high avalanche potential
Maps	Green Trails Nos. 79 and 80, Snowking Mountain and Cascade Pass; USGS 7.5-minute series, Downey Mountain and Huckleberry Mountain

Map —
page 99

This tour brings the skier to perfect early-season skiing terrain: broad, open heather slopes. In good weather you can see nearby

Mount Buckindy and Glacier Peak. An exposed ridge crossing provides reasonable access to the Mount Buckindy massif (2 to 3 days).

From Darrington drive north on the paved Darrington-Rockport road, crossing the Suiattle River in 6.5 miles. Continue east on the Suiattle River road (No. 26), and drive 17 miles to the Suiattle guard station. About 3.2 miles past the guard station, turn left onto the Green Mountain road (No. 2680) and continue for 6 miles. There is a Y in the road at 3400 feet. Take the left fork and drive to the trailhead (3800 feet). If the road is blocked lower down, simply park your car and hike or ski the road to the trailhead.

Follow the trail north for 1.5 miles until you reach a wide avalanche track. Ascend the left side of this track, keeping to the trees. Cross the slope near its top, moving east above a small rib. From this rib, contour north and east to the summit of Green Mountain (4 miles from the trailhead). It is feasible to tour slopes adjacent to Green Mountain if slopes are stable. Return to the car by reversing the approach.

Do not attempt this tour if a warming trend is expected, or in any kind of avalanche conditions. If the road is closed, the tour becomes considerably longer.

Green Mountain in early season (Photo: Kerry Ritland).

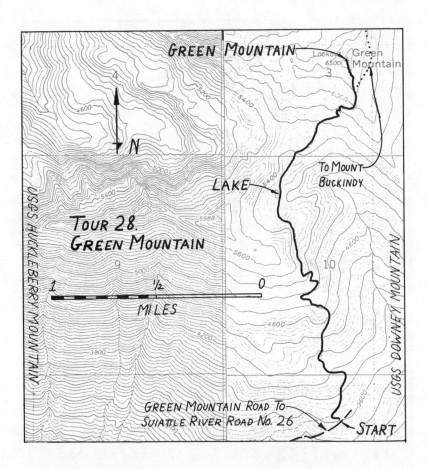

GREEN MOUNTAIN

TOUR 28.
GREEN MOUNTAIN

LAKE

TO MOUNT BUCKINDY

GREEN MOUNTAIN ROAD TO SUIATTLE RIVER ROAD No. 26

START

N

MILES
1   ½   0

USGS HUCKLEBERRY MOUNTAIN

USGS DOWNEY MOUNTAIN

DOME GLACIER

29

Map —
page 100

Start Point	Downey Creek Trailhead, 1400 feet
High Point	Spire Col, 7760 feet
Best Time	April to July
Length	3 to 5 days; 36 miles; 24 hours
Difficulty	Advanced; glacier travel; high avalanche potential
Maps	Green Trails No. 80, Cascade Pass; USGS 7.5-minute series, Dome Peak and Downey Mountain

Rarely seen Dome Peak is the Monarch of the Cascade Crest north of Glacier Peak. Two large glaciers east of the peak, the Dana and the Dome, offer excellent spring skiing amid spectacular scenery. The

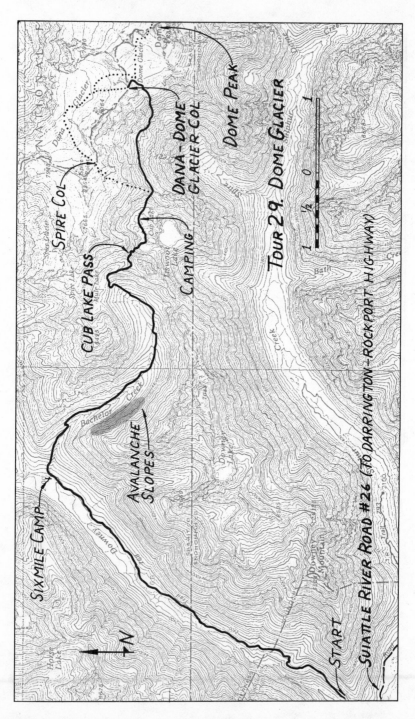

TOUR 29. DOME GLACIER

glaciers are crevassed but easily negotiable. Skiers will generally have little trouble avoiding crevasses. The approach to the Dome Peak area is long — 18 miles to the glacier — but its variety alleviates some of the misery of the hike.

Drive the Suiattle River road to Downey Creek Campground (20.5 miles from the Sauk River bridge, 1400 feet). The Downey Creek trail follows a deep glacial trough which heads in several large cirques. These cirques frequently release large avalanches that reach all the way to the valley's bottom. Use caution when traversing open areas.

The trail gains elevation rapidly, then levels out for the last 5 miles to Sixmile Camp. Cross footlogs to get to camp. This is a good spot to prepare for the morning hike.

East of Sixmile Camp is a waterfall stream, Bachelor Creek. The trail ascends this drainage, keeping generally north of the stream. Hike this trail for 7 miles, crossing a 6000-foot pass to get to Cub Lake (5300 feet). The larger Itswoot Lake lies about 500 feet lower and 0.2 mile south of Cub Lake. Beware of sluffs from open hillsides above. Descend to Cub Lake, traverse east to a bench just below Itswoot Ridge, and make camp. Itswoot Ridge is the rib descending southeast from Spire Point. Be sure your camp is located away from obvious avalanche runout zones.

Climb to a saddle (6200 feet) on Itswoot Ridge. From here you have a view of Dome Glacier and Dome Peak to the east, and Spire Point to the north.

To ski the Dome Glacier, descend the east side of the saddle, then contour left along snowfields to the glacier. From here you can climb Dome Peak via a col on its north ridge (optional). Climb to the col (8400 feet) just northeast of the true summit via steep snow (large moat). The summit may be reached from the col via a short but airy climb along a north ridge. See Fred Beckey's *Cascade Alpine Guide*, vol. 2 for details. The pointed spire seen from Itswoot Ridge is the lesser, southwest summit of Dome Peak.

An easier objective, and from a skiing perspective, a more productive one is to climb to the Dana-Dome glacier col, a broad saddle on the crest west of Dome Peak. There are reasonable camp spots here and both glaciers lie at your feet.

The Dana Glacier consists of two large lobes that are divided by a rocky, north-south rib. From Itswoot Ridge it is easiest to ski the western (leftmost) part. Climb snow slopes on the west (left) side of Itswoot Ridge to Spire Col (1 mile, 7760 feet). Some sections are steep — an ice ax is recommended. From the col simply cross over to the Dana Glacier. Ski the glacier, heading northeast. The glacier is moderately steep, lightly crevassed, and offers delightful skiing. When the skiing becomes hazardous below, regain Spire Col and return to camp.

If you have time, you could traverse to the rocky rib on your right (east) and traverse below it to reach the eastern lobe of the Dana Glacier. Once below (north of) the rib, turn right (east) and make a climbing southeast traverse for 0.3 mile, then climb south to the

Descending toward Agnes Creek (Photo: Gary Brill).

Dana-Dome glacier saddle (1.2 miles from rib, 7400 feet). Gain the saddle and traverse right (west) on the south side, heading back to Itswoot Ridge. Beware of sun-warmed snow on this southfacing slope. Total distance for this side trip is 6 miles.

This area is good even if you do not intend to do "grand tours." The snowy slopes of Itswoot Ridge and the various glaciers offer plenty of runs in a wilderness setting.

To return to the car, simply retrace the approach. There are some advantages to doing this tour in early season. The primary benefit is that you can ski out much of the lengthy approach. The risk, a real one, is that the sun-warmed slopes that flank Downey and Bachelor creeks will slide.

Downey Creek is also the exit for the Ptarmigan Traverse, a high route starting at Cascade Pass. This advanced tour can be done in four days in good conditions. It involves routefinding, steep glacier skiing, high avalanche potential, and exquisite scenery.

WHITEHORSE MOUNTAIN

30

Start Point	387th Avenue N.E., Niederprum Trailhead, 700 feet	
High Point	Whitehorse Mountain, 6852 feet	
Best Time	February to May	
Length	Day trip; 7 miles; 10 hours	
Difficulty	Advanced; glacier travel; navigation; high avalanche potential	
Maps	Green Trails No. 110, Silverton; USGS 15-minute series, Silverton	

Map— page 104

Whitehorse is one of the more spectacular outposts of the Cascade Range. It is also one of the few alpine ski ascents with a street address. The northern flank, visible from State Route 530, has been skied but is a risky descent with many cliff bands and considerable avalanche danger. The northwestern shoulder to Lone Tree Pass offers a good tour with a minimum of bushwhacking. Stable conditions and a reasonable snowpack above 3000 feet are required for this tour. Take ice axes and crampons.

Drive State Route 530 toward Darrington. West of Darrington 5 miles, at the Whitehorse store, take 387th Avenue N.E. south (turn right if coming from Burlington). Drive for 1.5 miles to Whitehorse trail No. 653 and take the trail to Niederprum Spring Campground. The path climbs for 2 miles, emerging from timber near 3200 feet, and ending near 4200 feet in a snow-covered avalanche zone. Climb directly up the steep slope (brushy in summer) for a few hundred feet, weaving around several gullies.

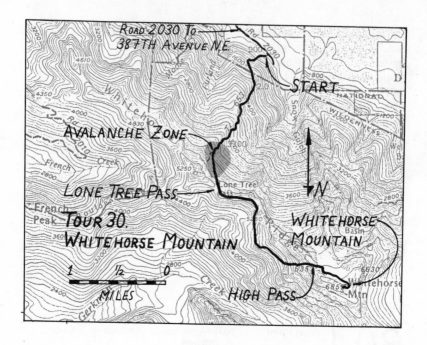

Traverse southeast toward Lone Tree Pass (4800 feet), picking the safest route through the cornices at the pass (4750 feet). From the pass, head east along the south side for about 0.5 mile, climbing over or around several minor obstacles along the way. A large rock tower seemingly blocks further progress. Descend a gully for 400 feet to reach the base of these ramparts. Make a climbing traverse to the southeast, turning a corner through a steep patch of timber. On leaving the trees, descend a few feet to a bench near 4600 feet that runs southeast, parallel to the ridge above. Follow this bench for 0.3 mile until you come to a steep snow gully. Climb this gully directly to High Pass. Remember: This snow slope can become unstable in warm afternoon sun. You should also beware of falling ice from rocks above.

High Pass is the entrance to the Whitehorse Glacier. Ski through a wind-formed corridor, then make a southeast climbing traverse up the glacier to reach the summit. Keep well to the east to avoid several steep wind rolls on the glacier. You can ski to within 100 feet of the summit. The final section is steep and exposed and requires an ice ax (and possibly crampons).

The view from the summit makes the approach seem worthwhile, and the descent is icing on the cake. Ski down to 6000 feet (head for town), then traverse back to High Pass. Use caution in descending the gully below High Pass and again on the slopes below Lone Tree Pass. Be sure not to descend too far in the woods below High Pass, before regaining the trail.

Skiing the Whitehorse Glacier — Tour 30 (Photo: Gary Brill).

MOUNT PILCHUCK

31

Start Point	Mount Pilchuck State Park Road, 3000 feet
High Point	Mount Pilchuck, 5324 feet
Best Time	January to March
Length	Day trip; 4 miles; 3 to 5 hours
Difficulty	Advanced; moderate avalanche potential
Maps	Green Trails No. 109, Granite Falls; USGS 15-minute series, Granite Falls

Mount Pilchuck is the western outrigger of the Cascades between Mount Baker and Snoqualmie Pass. It affords the skier a panoramic view of the western slope of the range from Mount Baker to Mount Rainier. This tour is feasible only when there is enough snow to ensure good skiing.

Drive State Route 92 east from Granite Falls. Past the Verlot ranger station 1 mile, turn right on the Mount Pilchuck State Park road (Road No. 42) and drive until snow or road conditions prevent further progress.

Depending on where the driving ended, skiers can either follow the road to the site of the abandoned ski area (2 to 4 miles, 3200 feet), or ski uphill (south or southwest), taking shortcuts through deep woods until the former ski area is reached.

From the ski-area parking lot it is 2 miles and 2100 feet to the

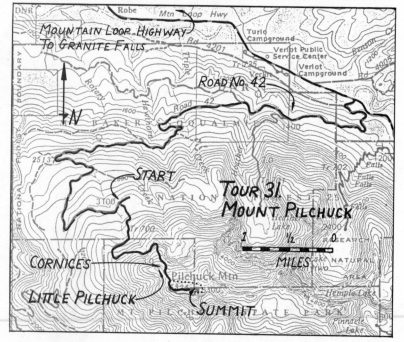

summit. Ski due south, passing "Little Pilchuck" (about 4400 feet) on the left, to a saddle. Beware of cornices drooping from the summit of this satellite.

From the saddle, ski up the southwest slopes to the summit. Avoid approaching the edge of the ridge too closely; huge cornices form over the north slope and can break off far back from the edge. Descend the route of ascent.

STEVENS PASS HIGHWAY, U.S. 2

The Stevens Pass highway provides a fast approach to year-around skiing in the North-Central Cascades. Most of the tours in this area are concentrated east of the Cascade Crest and tend to enjoy slightly drier weather than westside tours. All the tours in this area reached from primary roads are accessible all year. Those tours reached via secondary or back roads are sometimes accessible only in early or late season. Included in this section are tours in adjacent subranges—namely the Chiwaukum, Entiat, and Stuart ranges—all of which can be conveniently reached from U.S. 2 or U.S. 97.

This area is of great interest to skiers, topographically speaking. Slopes tend to be slightly gentler than those farther north, and elevations tend to be higher than those to the south. The result is snow and terrain that is well suited to backcountry skiing.

MOUNT HINMAN

32

Start Point	East Fork Foss River Road, 1600 feet
High Point	Mount Hinman, 7492 feet
Best Time	May to June
Length	Overnight; 20 miles; 14 hours
Difficulty	Advanced; glacier skiing; high avalanche potential
Maps	Green Trails Nos. 175 and 176, Skykomish and Stevens Pass; USGS 7.5-minute series, Mount Daniel and Big Snow

Map— page 108

Mount Hinman is a massive plateau, superficially similar to Bacon Peak, Snowking, and its own immediate neighbor, Mount Daniel. Although of moderate altitude, its broad plateau collects large amounts of snow and ice. This glacial cap offers ideal touring, with sweeping vistas, in a remote setting. There are three main approaches to the peak. One, described in this guide, follows the Foss River road from U.S. 2, then climbs south and east to gain the Hinman Plateau. The other two approaches are made via Interstate

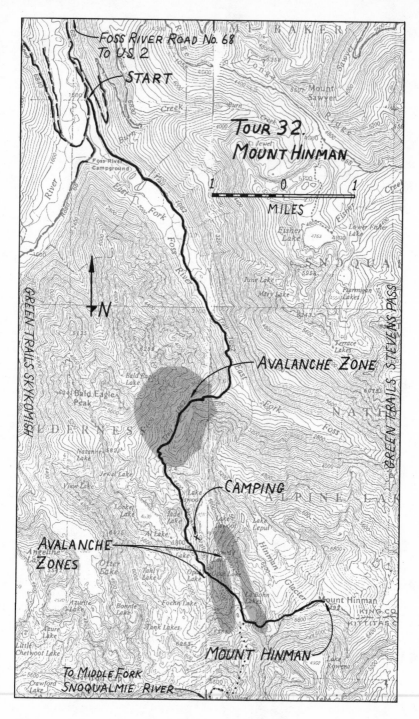

90 and either the Middle Fork Snoqualmie River or over Mount Daniel from the Salmon la Sac side. Mount Hinman is a good spring tour, made feasible by long days, clear approach roads, and stable slopes. Winter ascents are possible but dangerous.

Drive U.S. 2 east 1.8 miles from the town of Skykomish. Turn right on the Foss River road (No. 68) and turn right again in 1.2 miles. Continue driving until you reach the East Fork Foss River trailhead, about 4.3 miles from the highway.

Hike or ski the East Fork trail along the left (north) side of the river. The general direction of travel in this section is southeast. In about 4 miles head south. Cross the river in 4.6 miles (2100 feet) and turn right, heading west up a drainage below a huge cliff to your left. The trail keeps to the north side of the creek and turns south again in 0.5 mile as the angle eases off. This valley is very exposed to slides from Bald Eagle Peak to the right and the ridge on the left.

Continue climbing up the valley, heading south. Climb a steep headwall, then go through a defile to reach the hanging Necklace Valley (4600 feet). The valley contains Jade, Emerald, Opal, and Cloudy lakes. The maintained trail ends at Opal Lake, (8.3 miles, 4800 feet). There are good campsites in Necklace Valley. Camp away from the lakes and well away from slopes that could discharge snow onto your campsite.

Make an eastward climbing traverse from Opal Lake, heading to La Bohn Lakes (0.7 mile, 5800 feet). Just south of the largest lake is a small hump. Skirt the southwest side of the lake, pass the hump, then ski up the left side of the shoulder to the east.

Continue climbing until you reach the northeast ridge above you. Follow this ridge to the summit area. There are three main options from here: Ski the Hinman Glacier to the north; ski the Lynch Glacier to the northeast; or traverse east to the summit of Mount Daniel 2 miles away. The last alternative is a complicated traverse. See Fred Beckey's *Cascade Alpine Guide,* Vol. 1, for details.

The most certain descent retraces your approach. A descent route via Hinman Glacier to the creek below is untested. Cliffs below seem to make this route impractical.

A high traverse from La Bohn Lakes to Marmot Lakes over Mount Daniel has been done. Because of the steep-sided valleys in this area, stable conditions are required for tours here. Be especially wary of long periods of very hot weather.

Another fine early- or late-season tour is Tonga Ridge. This tour uses the same approach as the northern route to Mount Hinman, with a left turn up road No. 6830, 3.6 miles from the main highway. Follow road signs marked "Tonga Ridge" to the trailhead, then ski 1 mile south through forest to the meadows of Tonga Ridge. This is an advanced tour because of steep trail skiing and moderate avalanche potential.

COWBOY MOUNTAIN

33

Start Point	Top of Seventh Heaven Chair Lift, 5700 feet
High Point	Cowboy Mountain, 5700 feet
Best Time	December to April
Length	Day trip; 1.5 miles; 1 hour to ski area
Difficulty	Intermediate; moderate avalanche potential
Map	USGS 7.5-minute series, Stevens Pass

This tour is accessible for anybody with alpine ski equipment; simply ride the lifts to the top of the Seventh Heaven chair, and ski the "backside" of Cowboy Mountain. While navigation is not a problem on this tour, avalanche danger is; parties must be equipped to effect self-rescue. Check at the Stevens Pass avalanche control center for snow and avalanche conditions and follow the recommendations.

From the top of the Seventh Heaven chair lift, make a climbing traverse southwest around the right side of the summit of Cowboy Mountain (0.3 mile). Just past the summit, ski due south for 0.1 mile and 400 vertical feet, then head slightly east and down to a drainage, avoiding several small cliffs and deep ravines. Follow the stream south, staying out of the gully, then west to the highway to meet your ride back to the pass. This tour is only worthwhile with a good snowpack. Extremely dense timber, exposed stumps and brush make it a horror show in low-snowpack years.

Another good ski-area tour involves an ascent of the Tye–Mill Creek chair lift, then a descent of the far side of the mountain (the

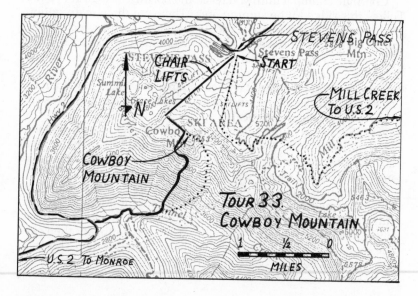

southeast shoulder of the ridge connecting Big Chief and Cowboy mountains). Descend to the power lines, then make a left turn and follow the hum down to the Mill Creek Sno-Park (4 miles). It is about 7 miles back to Stevens Pass from this Sno-Park, so be sure to arrange a return ride in advance.

Take a suitable wax kit and watch out for snowmobiles. Again, check with the avalanche control people before setting out.

HEATHER RIDGE

34

Start Point	Stevens Pass Summit Parking Lot, 4060 feet
High Point	Heather Ridge, 5400 feet
Best Time	December to March
Length	Day trip; 3 miles; 3 to 5 hours
Difficulty	Advanced; high avalanche potential
Maps	Green Trails Nos. 144, 145, 176, and 177, Benchmark Mountain, Wenatchee Lake, Stevens Pass, and Chiwaukum Mountains; USGS 7.5-minute series, Labyrinth Mountain and Stevens Pass

*Map—
page 112*

Heather Ridge is the mountain directly across U.S. 2 from the Stevens Pass ski area. It is unmarked on USGS maps. It is sometimes (erroneously) called "Skyline Ridge," perhaps after Skyline Lake, a small body of water near the summit. This short tour is a pleasant alternative to riding the lifts at the Stevens Pass ski area. There are both intermediate and advanced ski runs, and the north and southeast slopes of Heather Ridge frequently have untracked powder. There are plenty of other areas to explore too. Check with the avalanche control people at Stevens Pass to help determine the safety of the tour. The open trees on the right (east) side of Heather Ridge

*Approaching the open eastern slopes of northern Heather Ridge
(Photo: Donal O'Sullivan).*

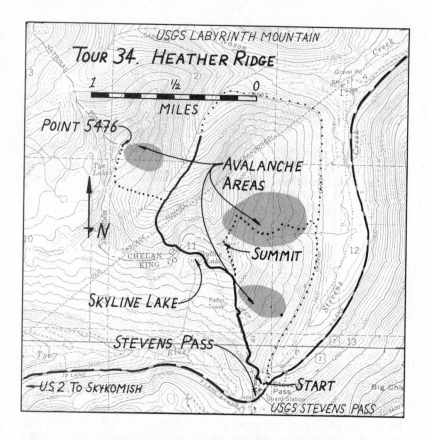

offer fabulous powder skiing, but lie on a slope that is subject to wind-loading and frequent avalanches.

The trail begins behind and left of the power substation at the northeast corner of the ski-area parking lot on the north side of U.S. 2. The trail (actually a maintenance road) winds up the hill (north) until it breaks out into clearings. If there are any indications of instability, turn around and go lift skiing. Otherwise continue, staying as close as practical to the ridge crest as you climb the open slope.

Near the top of the hill, head west until you reach Skyline Lake (5092 feet, 1.5 miles from the parking lot). The skiing is just over the hill northwest of the lake. From ridge crest, you can make numerous runs of up to 1000 vertical feet of skiing through open, old-growth timber. Good intermediate skiing is found on the slopes immediately around Skyline Lake.

Descents can be made either by reversing the approach, skiing out Nason Creek (see map), or by descending the east end of Heather Ridge. For the latter alternative, climb directly over the summit of

Heather Ridge via its south ridge. From the summit, head north for 0.3 mile along the narrow crest until you reach a low spot in the ridge where the slope angle eases off. Ski the fall line for 1500 feet until the terrain forces you left. Bushwhack the last 300 feet to a road which returns to the pass. This last alternative requires low avalanche hazard (it follows the path of the 1971 Yodelin avalanche) but offers a spectacular run.

From the north face of Heather Ridge, you can see the gleaming slopes of Point 5476 farther to the northwest. Its eastern flank offers good, but steep runs. Its major drawbacks are its lee aspect (large avalanches occur here) and the occasional presence of deep, man-eating moats in late spring. Nevertheless, this is a good objective in the right conditions.

YODELIN

35

Start Point	Stevens Pass Highway, 2700 feet
High Point	"Yodelin" Ridge, 5000 feet
Best Time	January to March
Length	Day trip; 4 miles; 4 hours
Difficulty	Intermediate; moderate avalanche potential
Maps	Green Trails No. 144, Benchmark Mountain; USGS 7.5-minute series, Stevens Pass and Labyrinth Mountain

Map— page 114

Yodelin was both a residential development and ski area just east of Stevens Pass. The homes are located north of U.S. 2 while the ski area, now defunct, lies just across the road. This short tour climbs the ridge east of the ski area and offers fine powder runs with little time commitment. It is basically an uphill road trip followed by downhill runs through clearcuts; an aerobic, but not exhausting, little tour.

Drive U.S. 2 3.3 miles east of Stevens Pass to a small plowed area on the eastbound lanes of the highway (room for four cars). Ski west along a snow-covered road, taking the first left turn available. Continue skiing the road past another switchback and through a large clearcut. Follow the road around another switchback left into a mature forest remnant. Continue heading east for 0.5 mile to a junction. At this point you have a choice of routes. Those inclined toward gentler touring may follow a switchback west (right) through a clearcut toward a broad saddle near 4800 feet. This saddle lies due south of the trailhead. From the saddle, you can make a direct descent to the car.

For a circle tour, skiers can traverse west from the saddle toward Big Chief Mountain, keeping near the ridge crest. In 0.6 mile, de-

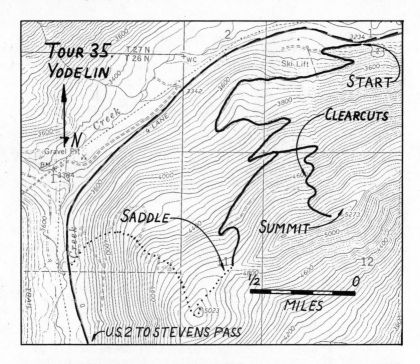

scend northwesterly through the abandoned Yodelin ski area toward U.S. 2, and then return along the highway.

To ski the steep and deep stuff, head east for 0.5 mile from the junction instead of turning west. Stay on the road until you come to the right edge of another clearcut (about 4100 feet).

Climb to the top of this clearcut (5000 feet). The ridge top is a few hundred feet to the south in deep woods (5200 feet).

Across the valley and to the southwest you can see some of the slopes of Heather Ridge. Northwest lies Lichtenberg Mountain and Jove Peak (Tour 36). Begin the descent by skiing the fall line (600 feet, steep) through the clearcut and into deep woods. Continue descending through the trees until, in 300 feet, you come out into another clearcut.

Make a rightward descending traverse into more woods until you come to a logging road. Be careful of the short but steep uphill bank above the road. Turn right on the road and ski it 300 feet to another clearcut. Descend the clearcut until you approach its lower edge, then enter a jumble of blown-down trees on its lower left (west) side. Continue descending, heading slightly left through dense trees, until you come to a streambed. Descend the streambed until you intersect a road, then ski the road to the car.

The bushwhack near the bottom of the final clearcut is horrible, but deep snowpack levels ease the pain considerably. There may be alternative escapes toward the right (east) side of the clearcut but these have not been tested by the author.

JOVE PEAK

36

Map—
page 116

Start Point	Stevens Pass Highway, 3100 feet
High Point	Jove Peak, 6007 feet
Best Time	December to April
Length	Day trip; 9 miles; 6 hours
Difficulty	Advanced; high avalanche potential
Maps	Green Trails No. 144, Benchmark Mountain; USGS 7.5-minute series, Labyrinth Mountain

Jove Peak lies about 2.5 miles north of Lichtenberg Mountain and is approached via the Smith Brook road. Its northwest and southeast shoulders can offer powder and corn on the same day! On the down side, afternoon slides from Union Peak pose a significant threat to skiers.

Drive U.S. 2 to the Smith Brook road turnoff, 4.5 miles east of Stevens Pass. Park well off the highway in the plowed area 300 feet east of the actual road. Ski the Smith Brook road, coming to clearcuts and switchbacks in 1.8 miles. Ahead and to the north lie the open southern slopes of Union Peak, a proven avalanche generator.

Either ski the road or head directly up the hill (due north) toward Rainy Pass (4600 feet, 3.5 road miles from U.S. 2). Rainy Pass is a broad saddle that marks the western end of the Nason Ridge trail (No. 1583) and the ridge bearing that name.

Descend the Rainy Creek drainage just east of the pass for 0.2 mile, then make a northwest-heading traverse toward Jove Peak, 1.2 miles to the northwest. Be certain that the steep hillside to your left is stable before heading across.

Continue the traverse through bands of old-growth trees, then ascend to the saddle between Union and Jove peaks (5100 feet). From the saddle, ski the southwest face of Jove to the summit (steep, open slopes). Make absolutely certain that these slopes are stable before committing to this face. If there is any doubt about slope stability, stay near Rainy Pass and ski the sheltered slope on the northwest side of the saddle.

From the summit of Jove you may ski west to Lake Janus or south back to Rainy Pass and out to the highway via the approach. An alternate route descends from Jove Peak to Lake Janus, then heads south along the trail and over Union Gap (2 miles, 600 feet elevation gain). This route has interesting views but greater exposure to avalanches.

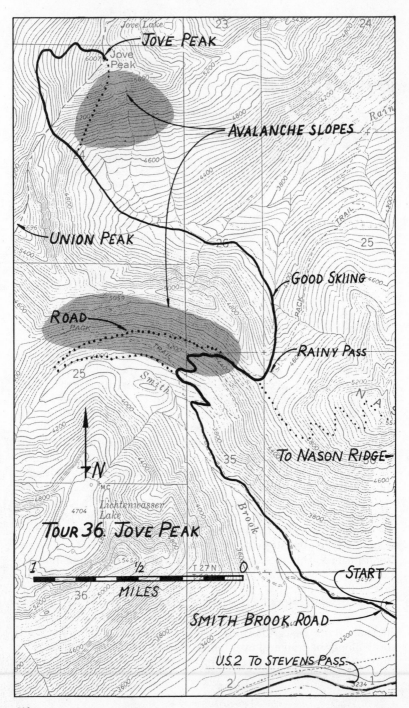

JOVE PEAK

AVALANCHE SLOPES

UNION PEAK

GOOD SKIING

ROAD

RAINY PASS

TO NASON RIDGE

N

TOUR 36. JOVE PEAK

1   ½   0

MILES

START

SMITH BROOK ROAD

U.S. 2 TO STEVENS PASS

For either route, the run back to the car is pleasant and quick since most of it is slightly downhill. Take along a little wax for the level sections of road.

JIM HILL MOUNTAIN

37

Start Point	Mill Creek Road, 2900 feet
High Point	Jim Hill Mountain, 6765 feet
Best Time	January to April
Length	Day trip; 6 miles; 8 to 10 hours
Difficulty	Advanced; high avalanche potential
Maps	Green Trails Nos. 144, 176, and 177, Benchmark Mountain, Stevens Pass, and Chiwaukum Mountains; USGS 7.5-minute series, Skykomish 1 S.E., Stevens Pass, Chiwaukum 2 S.W., and Chiwaukum 3 N.E.

*Map—
page 120*

Jim Hill Mountain takes its name from an early-day railroad tycoon. The mountain is visible from U.S. 2, just south of the highway near the Lanham Lake Sno-Park. It is the major peak west of the Chiwaukum Range. This could be considered one of the better tours of the Stevens Pass area.

Jim Hill Mountain is similar to the Silver Star tour from the perspective of avalanche danger: A few inches of snow at lower elevations—say, between 3500 and 5000 feet—frequently translates into a foot or more on the northeast face of the mountain. Hard or soft

Jim Hill Mountain; the crucial notch is visible on the right (Photo: Gary Brill).

slab avalanches on these slopes would have dire consequences for skiers traversing them.

Drive U.S. 2 5.7 miles east from Stevens Pass to the Sno-Park area adjacent to the highway (south side). If you are coming from Leavenworth, cross from the westbound lanes via an access road just after the highway department's maintenance shop. The Sno-Park is used by snowmobilers and bipeds alike. Be polite; where you're going, they can't begin to follow.

Ski up the Mill Creek road from the parking lot. Turn left at the first spur feeding into Mill Creek road and follow it for five switchbacks to the power lines. Turn right, skiing along the power-line trail until the slope just begins to drop toward Lanham Creek.

Ski uphill into the woods, traversing slightly left to meet an abandoned logging road a hundred feet above the east side of Lanham Creek. Follow this overgrown road for 1 mile, then continue for another mile along the now open Lanhan Creek drainage. Begin a climbing traverse before reaching Lanham Lake. The first few hundred feet above the lake are very steep. If the snow is sun-crusted, you may need to remove your skis for the ascent. Once above the steepest lower section, contour back and forth on benches to reach the saddle (5650 feet) on the north ridge of Jim Hill Mountain. You can obtain a good overview of the route from the northwest shore of Lanham lake.

Climb from the saddle on or to the right of the corniced ridge bounding the giant northeast bowl. The safest entrance into the bowl can be made via a small notch near 6400 feet, where the slope has a more windward aspect and consequently less slab-avalanche danger. Do not enter this bowl in any but low-avalanche-hazard conditions. Even then, look carefully for signs of instability.

The bowl offers runs ranging in length from 1200 to 2400 feet, depending on the snowpack and how high you decide to climb. You will need an ice ax, and possibly crampons, to reach the summit.

When the snowpack is thin, the skiing gets rough below 5200 feet, with many small trees and cliff near 4600 and 4300 feet. The cliff bands are skiable even under these conditions but require greater routefinding and some luck.

At the bottom of the bowl you have two options: climb back up to the saddle at 6400 feet, or exit via Henry Creek. The latter is the preferred choice only if there are three or more feet of snow at the highway (it's easy to check before setting out on the tour).

Henry Creek lies in a steep-sided ravine. Descend the drainage to 4100 feet and traverse left (west) for 0.5 mile. By now you should be around a corner of the ridge west of Henry Creek. Descend this steep ridge to the road and do not, under any circumstances, descend to the streambed. Henry Creek is about 15 minutes away from the Lanham Creek Sno-Park.

Descending to Henry Creek from Jim Hill Mountain (Photo: Gary Brill).

The other return involves retracing the approach. While this is a more certain route, it has little to recommend it because of the steepness of the terrain and the closeness of the trees. It's much better to wait until the snowpack is deep enough to make a roundtrip.

It has been reported that the Henry Creek descent route is also the most direct approach to the northeast face of Jim Hill Mountain. Park at the plowed parking area near the east railroad tunnel entrance and climb through awkward timber until the open slopes below the face are gained.

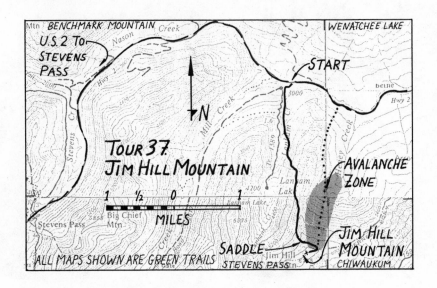

ROCK MOUNTAIN

38

Map — page 122

Start Point	Stevens Pass Highway, 2700 feet
High Point	Rock Mountain, 6852 feet
Best Time	October to November; April to May
Length	Day trip; 9 miles; 6 hours
Difficulty	Advanced; high avalanche potential
Maps	Green Trails No. 145, Wenatchee Lake; USGS 15-minute series, Wenatchee Lake

Rapid access, a scenic hike, and open slopes make the Rock Mountain tour delightful after an early-season snowfall above 5000 feet. The heather benches and smooth scree slopes require little snow to provide excellent skiing with little avalanche danger. Later in

Firnspiegel on Mount Howard (Photo: Marilyn Lindahl).

the season, large open slopes are dangerous to ski except in very stable conditions. This tour is an escape route from the Nason Ridge tour. Take ice axes and crampons.

Drive U.S. 2 over Stevens Pass. Rock Mountain trail No. 1587 begins on the north side of the highway, 9 miles east of the summit. Hike the trail for 4 miles to the ridge above Rock Lake. If the trail is snow covered, take ice axes since the lower parts of the trail are steep and exposed. The trail ascends the north–south-trending ridge to Rock Lake basin. In mid-to-late season this ridge can be heavily corniced.

Rock Lake is set in a basin with open slopes facing north, south, and east. Surely you can find skiing on one of these slopes (when the avalanche hazard is low)! Be certain to allow enough time to hike out in daylight since the trail traverses cliff bands near the trailhead. From the crest above Rock Lake, you may elect to ski to the summit of Rock Mountain or ski the open slopes above the lake. Schilling Creek has been skied directly to the highway in exceptionally heavy snow years. This should only be attempted when the snowpack is well frozen and the weather is cool and stable.

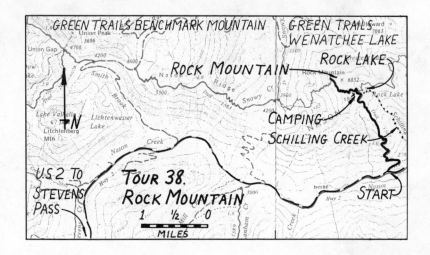

MOUNT HOWARD

39

Map—
page 124

Start Point	Merritt Lake Trail, 2600 feet
High Point	Mount Howard, 7063 feet
Best Time	December to March
Length	Day trip; 11 miles; 7 to 9 hours
Difficulty	Advanced; high avalanche potential
Maps	Green Trails No. 145, Wenatchee Lake; USGS 15-minute series, Wenatchee Lake

Mount Howard is the high point of Nason Ridge and offers outstanding skiing both in mid- and late winter. There is avalanche danger and skiers should be extremely careful to evaluate slope stability before venturing onto slopes. Take ice axes and crampons.

Drive U.S. 2 from Stevens Pass to the Merritt Lake trailhead (15 miles east of the pass). Hike or ski up the hill, trending generally northwest. As you approach 6000 feet, the hillside steepens to a ridge, becoming narrower near the top. Climb it on or left of the crest to avoid cornices.

As the ridge broadens again, continue climbing until the summit of Mount Mastiff (6741 feet) comes into view. Mount Howard lies 1

Sun-warmed snow sloughs on Mount Howard (Photo: Marilyn Lindahl).

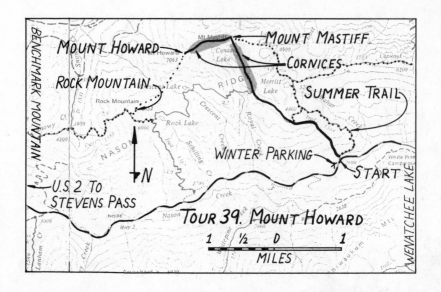

mile west and slightly south of Mount Mastiff. Ascend the open slope directly toward, and over Mastiff's summit, then on to Mount Howard. In some seasons this traverse is difficult because of cornice build-up. In that case, you should be prepared to turn around here.

The north bowl of Mount Howard is an exceptionally fine run, although the northeast ridge often sports a 30-foot cornice. An interesting tour can be made by climbing Mount Howard, then skiing its north face out to Wenatchee Lake. This tour involves miles of nearly level terrain along Wenatchee Lake and therefore is better suited to Nordic equipment.

NASON RIDGE

40

Start Point	Stevens Pass Highway, 2700 feet
High Point	Mount Howard, 7060 feet
Best Time	December to April
Length	Overnight; 26 miles; 14 hours
Difficulty	Advanced; navigation; high avalanche potential
Maps	Green Trails Nos. 144 and 145, Benchmark Mountain and Wenatchee Lake; USGS 7.5-minute series, Labyrinth Mountain and Wenatchee Lake

Map — page 126

A complete traverse of Nason Ridge is a magnificent tour offering grand views, challenging skiing, and a chance to do a complete traverse instead of the usual "out and back." This tour is relatively uncommitting since it's possible to escape in at least three places before the eastern end of the ridge. Avalanche hazard must be low to do this tour safely. Even then, always select your route to minimize this everpresent danger. The Nason Ridge traverse can be started at either end, but it is generally safer to start at the northwestern end because the steep slopes are easier (and safer) to ascend than to descend. Also, if the weather gets warmer, the descent route on the east end is safer than the descent from Rock Mountain to Snowy Creek. Take ice axes, crampons, and a wax kit for this tour.

Drive U.S. 2 to the Smith Brook road (see Tour 36). Ski the road to Rainy Pass, watching for slides from the south slope of Union Peak.

From the saddle, ski southeast along the west side of the ridge for 0.4 mile. When the hill steepens, switchback up to the ridgecrest (5500 feet). Ski along the winding crest for 1.8 miles, generally staying on the north side of the ridge. Watch for cornices—stay well back of their crowns. When the ridge narrows, descend the north side for 1200 feet toward the Snowy Creek drainage, trending east. As soon as possible, begin climbing the lightly wooded slopes to the east until you reach a saddle high on Rock Mountain (6000 feet, 6.8 miles from Rainy Pass). The summit of Rock Mountain lies 0.2 mile to the north, and Rock Lake lies 0.5 mile due east, and below. This saddle is not obvious on either Green Trails or USGS maps since it is essentially a low spot on the south ridge of Rock Mountain.

Here you must make a decision: Continue the tour, or descend. You can escape by retracing the approach or taking Rock Mountain's gullies or trail. To descend via the trail, make a descending traverse from the saddle, heading due east for 0.2 mile to a shoulder. When the broad rib gets steep, turn right (southeast) and ski through gentle meadows, keeping to the left of the steepening ridge (see Tour 38 for details). To descend Schilling Creek requires a deep snow pack and stable conditions since much of the descent takes place in a deep gully.

To continue the tour, first decide how much daylight you have left. If time is short, descend to the shoulder 0.2 mile to the east and camp. The lakeside and valley below may be more sheltered from wind but could become a trap if a warm storm moves in suddenly.

If you have more than 3 hours of daylight left and want to cover ground, climb the ridge on your left to the summit of Rock Mountain. Savor the views briefly, then descend the northeast ridge toward Mount Howard. Bypass steeper sections by moving left or right, depending on cornice buildup. Make camp at the saddle (about 6300 feet) above Crescent Lake, southwest of Mount Howard. It is best to abandon the tour if the weather is unstable since the open slopes of Mounts Howard and Mastiff may become hazardous. Do this by retracing your approach rather than continuing east.

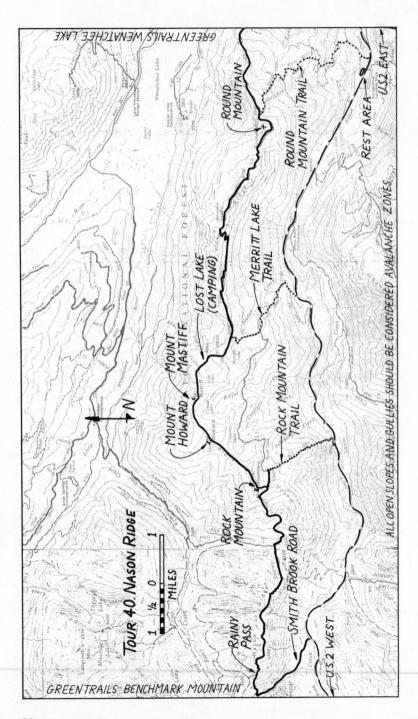

TOUR 40. Nason Ridge

MOUNT HOWARD

MOUNT MASTIFF

LOST LAKE (CAMPING)

ROUND MOUNTAIN

ROUND MOUNTAIN TRAIL

MERRITT LAKE TRAIL

ROCK MOUNTAIN TRAIL

ROCK MOUNTAIN

RAINY PASS

SMITH BROOK ROAD

U.S. 2 WEST

U.S. 2 EAST

REST AREA

N

MILES

GREENTRAILS WENATCHEE LAKE

GREENTRAILS BENCHMARK MOUNTAIN

ALL OPEN SLOPES AND GULLIES SHOULD BE CONSIDERED AVALANCHE ZONES.

To continue, make an ascending traverse northeast to the broad south slope of Mount Howard. Continue climbing until you reach the summit (7060 feet, 1 mile from the saddle). Descend the northeast slope of Howard, then ski the open western slope of Mount Mastiff to its summit (6741 feet).

Ski the east face of Mastiff, descending to Lost Lake (4900 feet) and crossing the frozen surface where the lake is narrowest. There is good camping at Lost Lake. The trail heads southeast from the south shore of the lake, up a hill and through a small pass (5400 feet) to the right of a small pinnacle. Descend southeast to Merritt Lake (5200 feet) and decide whether to escape or continue.

To escape, ski southeast 1 mile from the lake, then descend south-southeast. Stay out of the Mahar Creek drainage. The open trees and steep hill make for a fine descent to the highway (3.6 miles from the lake).

To continue the tour from Merritt Lake, make a climbing traverse, heading due east to the ridge top and Alpine Lookout (6200 feet, 2.6 miles from Merritt Lake). There are flat spots for camping here. The

Looking back to Rock Mountain from Mount Howard (Photo: Gary Brill).

lookout represents the final high point of the tour: It's all downhill from here. Follow the ridge east for 3 miles to Round Mountain, the eastern high point of Nason Ridge (5700 feet).

To return to U.S. 2, descend to the southeast for 1300 feet to intersect road No. 6910 and then follow it for 4 miles to the highway, just east of the rest area (closed in winter). Alternatively, you can ski southeast through timber until you reach the highway (2.9 miles from Round Mountain). This escape is a good alternative finish when road R290 along Wenatchee Lake is closed.

To finish the long traverse, descend the east slope of Round Mountain, staying close to the crest of the broad, timbered ridge. Continue the descent to Nason Creek Campground and ski the road to civilization. Since road conditions vary from year to year, make your tour plans after a personal review of conditions.

CHIWAUKUM MOUNTAINS

41

Start Point	Whitepine Road, 2800 feet	
High Point	Big Chiwaukum, 7900 feet	
Best Time	April to May	
Length	Day trip; 16 miles; 8 to 10 hours	
Difficulty	Intermediate; high traverses are advanced; high avalanche potential	
Maps	Green Trails Nos. 145 and 177, Wenatchee Lake and Chiwaukum Mountains; USGS 15-minute series, Wenatchee Lake and Chiwaukum Mountains	

This is a good tour because it provides easy access to the heart of the Chiwaukum Range via a scenic, if lengthy, approach. This tour has a fairly narrow "window" because of the nature of the terrain and the depth of the snowpack. The trail near the trailhead passes through a steep-sided gorge. If snow covers the trail, the skier or hiker is faced with a long, very steep traverse above a torrent in the gorge. One slip would end the tour. It's much better to wait until this section of trail melts out. The problem then is that the snowpack this far east of the Cascade Crest is thin and melts out quickly. Proper timing is important to maximize skiing. Take ice axes and crampons.

Drive U.S. 2 to the Whitepine Creek road No. 2638 (13.7 miles east of Stevens Pass). Drive past all side roads and under a railroad bridge to the road end at 3.2 miles (2800 feet). Hike the Whitepine Creek trail, taking great caution where it is eroded or snow covered.

In 2.5 miles (3200 feet) there is a fork. Take the left trail and head south up the Wildhorse drainage. The trail diverges from the creek, climbing swiftly to gentler slopes about 2.7 miles from the fork (4800

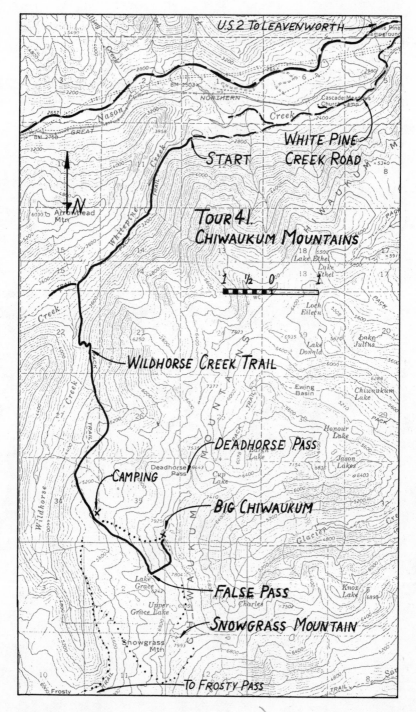

U.S. 2 To LEAVENWORTH

WHITE PINE CREEK ROAD

START

TOUR 41.
CHIWAUKUM MOUNTAINS

WILDHORSE CREEK TRAIL

DEADHORSE PASS

CAMPING

BIG CHIWAUKUM

FALSE PASS

SNOWGRASS MOUNTAIN

TO FROSTY PASS

feet). Deadhorse Pass lies a short distance above on the crest. Big Chiwaukum is the broad summit 1 mile south of Deadhorse Pass.

Ski past the sharp-crested ridge descending northwest from the summit area of Big Chiwaukum and camp near 5600 feet, due west of the peak. Excellent skiing can be found in the vicinity of this camp.

To climb Big Chiwaukum, traverse southeast across several ridge and gully systems to the open basin southwest of the summit. Climb steepening slopes directly up the headwall, or ascend south to a false pass at 6600 feet. From the pass, it is a rock climb to the summit. See Fred Beckey's *Cascade Alpine Guide*, Vol. 1, for details.

This area offers many fine runs in open bowls, but cliffy terrain makes high traverses on the west side of the range difficult. However, by keeping to the level of the trail, it is quite reasonable to reach good skiing in upper Wildhorse Creek. A long traverse over Frosty Pass would bring intrepid skiers to upper Icicle Creek.

The western slope of the Chiwaukum Range offers good spring skiing (Photo: Gary Brill).

It is not practical to reach the eastern slopes of Big Chiwaukum because cliffs guard the upper edges of the east-slope glaciers. However, the steep north face of Snowgrass Mountain can be reached traversing from the broad south ridge at 7000 feet. Descending the east side of Deadhorse Pass to the Chiwaukum or Glacier Creek drainage is untested.

MOUNT MAUDE

42

Map — page 132

Start Point	Phelps Creek Road, 3500 feet
High Point	Mount Maude, 9082 feet
Best Time	April to June
Length	2 to 3 days; 18 miles; 14 hours
Difficulty	Advanced; high avalanche potential; navigation
Map	USGS 15-minute series, Holden

The Entiat Mountains are rugged, remote, and tall. Mount Maude is one of the few nonvolcanic peaks in the state higher than 9000 feet. Its north face has not seen a ski descent, although rumor has it that this will have occurred before year's end. The gentle south shoulder is a more reasonable goal, one that can be done in a long weekend. Take ice axes, crampons, and a wax kit for the ski out.

Drive U.S. 2 to the Lake Wenatchee turnoff and turn east on State Route 207 toward Lake Wenatchee State Park. From the highway 4.5 miles is a three-way intersection. Go east on county road No. 22 for 1.4 miles to reach the Chiwawa road. The Plain Road (State Route 209) can be taken from Leavenworth to reach this location (18 miles). Drive the Chiwawa River road for 22 miles to the Phelps Creek road and turn right. Drive 2 miles, or as far as conditions permit, and park.

Hike the gently rolling Phelps Creek trail for 3.2 miles to the Leroy Creek trail (4100 feet), just north of Leroy Creek.

Leroy Creek trail will, with luck, be completely covered with snow. Ski or hike the steep shoulder north of the stream, heading east-northeast until the angle eases off near 5000 feet (about 1 mile). As you leave the thinning trees, you'll find yourself in a large cirque with the bulk of Mount Maude to the east and Seven-fingered Jack to the northeast. There is a broad bench with fine campsites above the steep section (2 miles from the confluence of Leroy and Phelps creeks). This slope often avalanches in afternoon sunshine. Continue heading northeast for 0.5 mile, then begin a southeast traverse toward the saddle (6600 feet) 1 mile to the south. There are level campsites near the saddle. From there, climb the ridge heading east to the south shoulder of Mount Maude. Gain the shoulder at a saddle, keeping left of a small gendarme. Ice Lakes lie just east and below the pass.

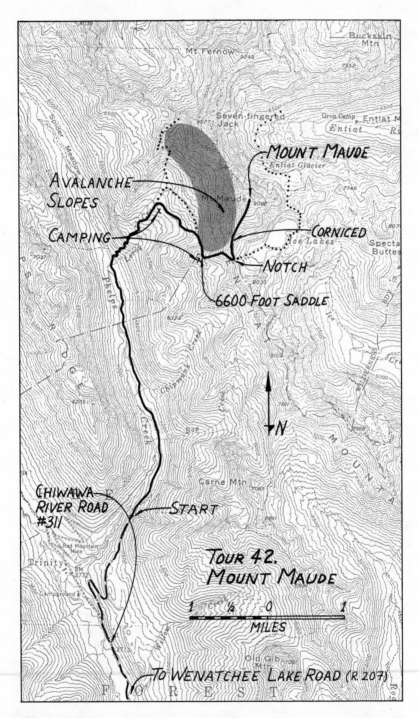

AVALANCHE SLOPES

CAMPING

MOUNT MAUDE

CORNICED

NOTCH

6600 FOOT SADDLE

CHIWAWA RIVER ROAD #311

START

TOUR 42.
MOUNT MAUDE

1   ½   0   1
MILES

TO WENATCHEE LAKE ROAD (R 207)

Climb north on the ridge, avoiding cornices on its eastern edge. The summit is easily gained in 1 mile. Do not tarry lest sun-warmed slopes become unstable. Return to camp and the car via your approach. Other good local objectives include the Entiat Glacier and the southwest basin of Seven-fingered Jack.

CHIWAWA MOUNTAIN

<table>
<tr><td rowspan="6">43

Map—
page 135</td><td>**Start Point**</td><td>Phelps Creek Road, 3500 feet</td></tr>
<tr><td>**High Point**</td><td>Chiwawa Mountain, 8460 feet</td></tr>
<tr><td>**Best Time**</td><td>April to June</td></tr>
<tr><td>**Length**</td><td>2 to 3 days; 19 miles; 15 hours</td></tr>
<tr><td>**Difficulty**</td><td>Advanced; glacier travel; high avalanche potential</td></tr>
<tr><td>**Maps**</td><td>USGS 15-minute series, Holden and Wenatchee Lake</td></tr>
</table>

Chiwawa Mountain lies at the head of the Chiwawa River and offers good skiing and spectacular views of Bonanza Peak. The approach is the same as that of Mount Maude (see Tour 42) until you cross Leroy Creek.

Continue past Leroy Creek, heading up Phelps Creek to Spider Meadow (5000 feet). Camp here, or switchback up the headwall to the west and gain the Spider Glacier. Ascend the glacier, reaching Spider Col (7100 feet) in 0.7 mile.

From the saddle, make a descending traverse to the northwest, then contour west across the Lyman Glacier for 0.3 mile to the southwest. The summit lies 1.5 miles southwest of the col. To ski above 7000 feet on this glacier requires low avalanche-hazard conditions. Climb southwest, past a steep section near 7300 feet (crevasses), then head directly for the summit. In most years the summit involves a class 3 scramble.

Plan your descent carefully since the convex glacier makes crevasses hard to see from above. If you are near the summit ridge, you could drop over and ski the southwest ridge to 6500 feet, then contour southeast along Red Mountain until you converge on an abandoned mining road (shown as a trail on maps). Follow the trail (6000 feet) south, then east, across Phelps Ridge to Phelps Creek.

A classic tour, first done in May 1938, involves a ski ascent of North Star Mountain. Ski the Lyman Glacier to Lyman Lake, then climb northeast past Cloudy Peak to the Cloudy-North Star Saddle. The summit, 0.6 mile away to the northeast (8068 feet) has close-up views of Bonanza Peak, the highest nonvolcanic mountain in Washington.

For a more conservative tour, ski the Lyman Glacier until you can ski no more, then return to camp and the car by retracing your approach. The descent from Spider Col is sheer delight: a moderate run in a wilderness setting followed by miles of rolling, generally downhill, skiing.

Approaching the snout of the Lyman Glacier (Photo: Gary Brill).

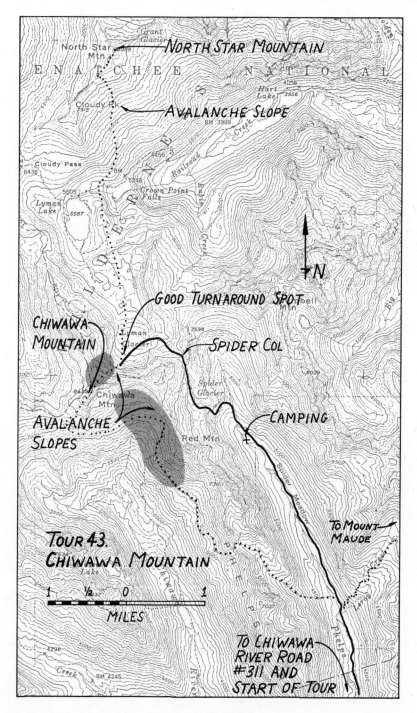

NORTH STAR MOUNTAIN

AVALANCHE SLOPE

N

GOOD TURNAROUND SPOT

CHIWAWA MOUNTAIN

SPIDER COL

AVALANCHE SLOPES

CAMPING

TOUR 43.
CHIWAWA MOUNTAIN

1   ½   0   1
MILES

TO MOUNT MAUDE

TO CHIWAWA RIVER ROAD #311 AND START OF TOUR

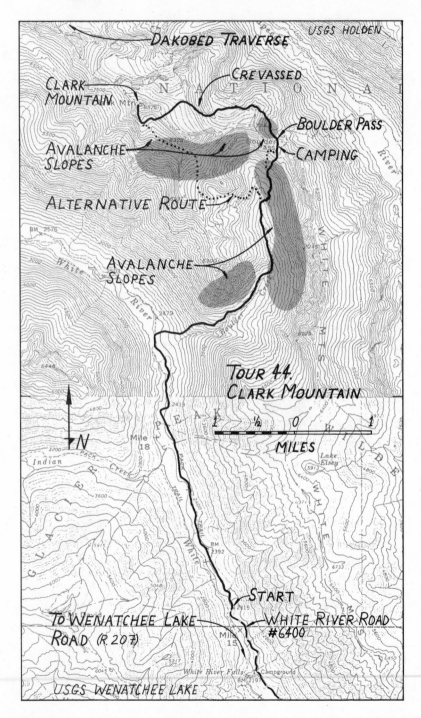

DAKOBED TRAVERSE

USGS HOLDEN

CREVASSED

CLARK MOUNTAIN

BOULDER PASS

CAMPING

AVALANCHE SLOPES

ALTERNATIVE ROUTE

AVALANCHE SLOPES

TOUR 44. CLARK MOUNTAIN

N

MILES

START

WHITE RIVER ROAD #6400

TO WENATCHEE LAKE ROAD (R.207)

USGS WENATCHEE LAKE

CLARK MOUNTAIN

44

Start Point	White River Road, 2300 feet
High Point	Clark Mountain, 8576 feet
Best Time	March to June
Length	2 to 3 days; 24 miles; 18 hours
Difficulty	Advanced; glacier travel; high avalanche potential
Maps	USGS 15-minute series, Holden and Wenatchee Lake

Clark Mountain enjoys a magnificent position west of the Napeequa drainage. It can be approached from either the White or Napeequa rivers, although the former approach eliminates two rather nasty fords required on the latter. The White River approach is described in this tour. (The Napeequa approach leaves the Chiwawa, crosses Little Giant Pass, then crosses the Napeequa to Boulder Pass.) The slopes of Clark Mountain are bare and avalanche swept. Take ice axes and crampons.

Drive past the Lake Wenatchee ranger station and continue 1.5 miles to a junction. Keep to the right, taking the White River road to its terminus (2300 feet).

Hike the near-level trail to its junction (4 miles, 2470 feet) with the Boulder Pass trail. The trail ascends the Boulder Creek drainage to its source near Boulder Pass. Ski up the open and avalanche-exposed basin of Boulder Creek to a headwall below Boulder Pass. Make this ascent during morning hours. The headwall is most easily climbed through small trees just east of where the trail is shown on the map.

Boulder Pass provides reasonable campsites with good skiing opportunities, even if you don't make a summit attempt. The high shoulder 0.7 mile northeast of Boulder Pass provides many outstanding runs, although some end in cliffs.

There are two routes to Clark Mountain's summit. The first approach climbs the moderately angled, but very active Walrus Glacier. A rope is advised here and late-season skiers may need some luck in crossing major crevasse systems.

From Boulder Pass climb up a shoulder to the northwest, contouring around this at 6800 feet to gain the Walrus Glacier. The flat area of the glacier near this elevation provides a crevasse-free ramp to the center of the glacier. The largest crevasses occur between 7100 and 7700 feet with a large bergschrund near 7700 feet. Ski up the center or left-center of the glacier to the east ridge of the summit. Cross over this ridge to the south slope and climb easily to the summit. Descend the approach route or the southeast slope (untested).

This latter route is also an untried ascent route. Begin at 5200 feet southwest of Boulder Pass. Climb to the northwest, passing Point

Crevasse and snow bridge on the Walrus Glacier (Photo: Gary Brill).

8373 at about 7700 feet. From here, climb directly northwest to the summit.

Make your return by retracing the approach route. Spend an extra day if the afternoon sun warms the snow excessively, to allow slopes to stabilize. This area is subject to very large slides.

ICICLE RIDGE

45

Start Point	Icicle River Road, 1200 feet
High Point	Icicle Ridge, 6800 feet
Best Time	December to February
Length	Day trip; 14 miles; 8 hours
Difficulty	Intermediate; loop tour is advanced; moderate avalanche potential
Maps	Green Trails Nos. 177 and 178, Chiwaukum Mountains and Leavenworth; USGS 15-minute series, Chiwaukum Mountains and Leavenworth

"Icicle" is the white man's interpretation of the native word *nasikelt* meaning "steep-sided canyon." The ridge forming the northern boundary of Icicle Canyon is indeed steep sided, but much of the

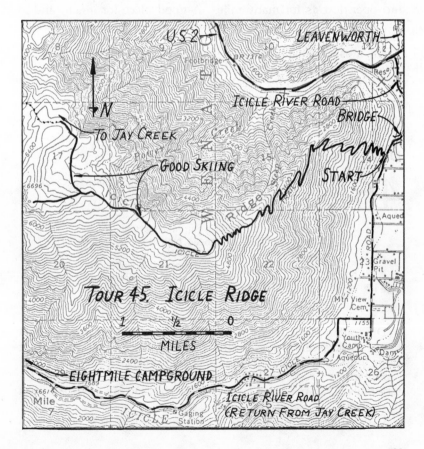

steepness can be avoided by climbing it lengthwise from east to west. Adequate snow cover is essential for an enjoyable tour. Since the southern exposure experiences rapid ablation of the snowpack, it is suggested that you make this tour in midwinter conditions, observing all avalanche precautions, of course. If the snow is too unstable, you can always go track skiing on the lovely tracks in Leavenworth.

Drive U.S. 2 to Leavenworth. On the west end of town, head south on the Icicle River road for 1.5 miles. The trail begins on the right side of the road just south of the Wenatchee River bridge. Parking may be difficult to find, but do not block driveways or park on the road or you will be towed.

Follow the trail up switchbacks on moderate slopes, or ski where you will, heading generally west. The forest is thin and you have views of the Leavenworth valley. Near 3000 feet you approach the ridge crest. Follow it southwest, continually gaining elevation until the angle begins to ease off near 5000 feet (3 miles from the road). The ridge begins to turn northwest and you can ski along gentle slopes and open forests for many miles. A good place for lunch, and a turnaround, is the junction of the Fourth of July and the Icicle Ridge trails (6800 feet, 6.8 miles from the road).

The most reasonable descent is made by retracing the approach. Less reasonable skiers have made circle tours by continuing 2.5 miles and descending near Jay Creek, then skiing out the Icicle River road to Leavenworth. This route is very steep.

DRAGONTAIL PEAK

46		
Start Point	Stuart Lake Trailhead (Mountaineer Creek Trail), 3400 feet
High Point	Dragontail Peak, 8840 feet
Best Time	April to May
Length	Overnight; 14 miles; 9 hours
Difficulty	Advanced; high avalanche potential
Maps	Green Trails Nos. 177 and 209, Chiwaukum Mountains and Mount Stuart; USGS 15-minute series, Chiwaukum Mountains and Mount Stuart

Map—
page 142

Dragontail Peak is the second-highest summit in the Stuart Range. A ski ascent is possible from the east side, above the 2500-foot slope to Asgaard Pass. This is a feasible tour because the road to the Mountaineer Creek trailhead melts out long before the skiing deteriorates. Crampons and ice axes advisable. Do not leave valuables in your car.

Drive the Icicle River road from Leavenworth to Bridge Creek

Descending from Asgaard Pass (Photo: Gary Brill).

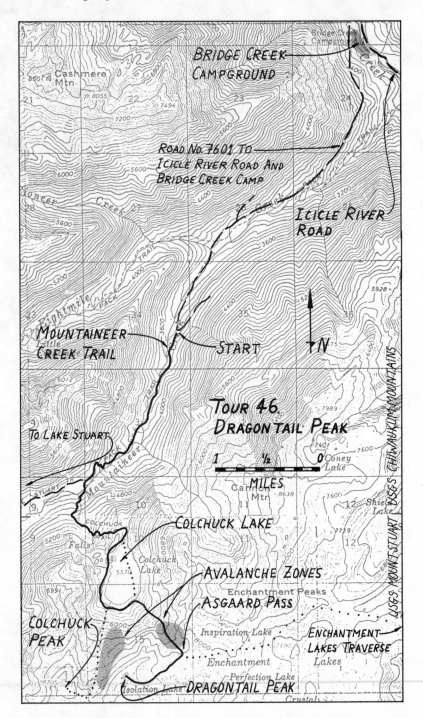

BRIDGE CREEK
CAMPGROUND

ROAD No. 7601 To
ICICLE RIVER ROAD AND
BRIDGE CREEK CAMP

ICICLE RIVER
ROAD

MOUNTAINEER
CREEK TRAIL

START

↑N

TOUR 46
DRAGONTAIL PEAK

TO LAKE STUART

1   ½   0   Coney
                    Lake
MILES

COLCHUCK LAKE

AVALANCHE ZONES

Enchantment Peaks
ASGAARD PASS

COLCHUCK
PEAK

Inspiration Lake

ENCHANTMENT
LAKES TRAVERSE

Enchantment   Lakes

Perfection Lake

DRAGONTAIL PEAK

Campground (14 miles), and cross the Icicle River on a concrete bridge. Continue driving the road for 4 miles, parking at a broad road elbow. Hike the Lake Stuart trail for 2.5 miles to a level valley with a beaver-dammed stream.

The Colchuck Lake trail forks left in this area and climbs 1.8 miles to the lake (5570 feet). Cross the stream on a footlog and hike south through boulders to the trail. The trail switchbacks up and over buttresses to approach the lake north of its outlet. The safest, best campsites are along the west side of the lake.

If the lake is not frozen well enough to permit skiing, circle the lake on the right, climbing over small humps, and then enter woods on the southwest shore. Continue through the woods and come out to an open basin. The northwest wall of Dragontail rises ahead and Colchuck Peak lies to the right.

It may be easier to ski along the frozen lake at this point rather than to wander through the boulder field. Either way, hike up the long slope toward Asgaard Pass (7800 feet). If there is significant new snow on the valley bottom, terminate the tour here. The slope could release when you are on it. Otherwise, it is easiest to ascend the slope on its left side to about 7200 feet, working right to a moraine to bypass cliffs and waterfalls above. Views begin to open as you ascend toward the pass and you'll get glimpses of the innards of the huge couloirs dividing the faces of Dragontail.

From the pass, begin heading southwest toward a steep glacier headwall. If there is significant fresh snow on the flat here, this headwall may have windslab on it. In that case, make alternative plans. Otherwise, climb the glacier (the right side may be easier) to the saddle. From the saddle, a gentle spur leads to the summit area 300 feet above. The summit is an undistinguished lump of rock but the views are incredible.

To descend, retrace your ascent. Ski the steep portions of Asgaard Pass carefully: It's steep. If it's icy, you may need to crampon down.

Colchuck Glacier is a good side trip if you have an extra afternoon. Instead of heading up Asgaard Pass, ascend the steep slopes to the terminal moraine below the glacier. Be careful of slab formation below the crest of the terminal moraine. The glacier segment below Colchuck peak is crevassed but the snowfield adjacent to Dragontail is relatively crevasse free (watch out for avalanches and rockfalls). Climb this steep slope to Colchuck Col (8000 feet). The summit is a steep 700-foot scramble away, which is not recommended. The south slope of the col is very steep at first, then eases off slightly in the Porcupine Creek drainage. It has been skied, but it should be attempted only when avalanche danger is low (see the next tour). A traverse of the Enchantment Lakes can be made via Asgaard Pass. There are, however, avalanche paths on both the entrance and exit of this high route.

PORCUPINE CREEK

47

Start Point	Ingalls Creek Trailhead, 1950 feet
High Point	Colchuck Col, 8000 feet
Best Time	March to May
Length	Overnight; 20 miles; 14 hours
Difficulty	Advanced; high avalanche potential
Maps	Green Trails No. 209, Mount Stuart; USGS 15-minute series, Mount Stuart

The long Ingalls Creek valley is bisected in many places by huge avalanche slopes from the flanking mountainsides. One of these

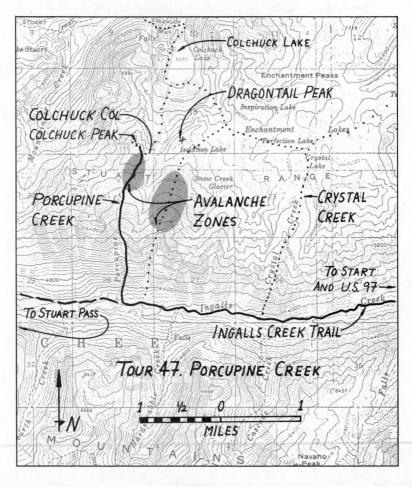

slopes, the Porcupine drainage, is noteworthy because it not only offers good skiing, but it also tops out in an interesting place, Colchuck Col. Ideal conditions here consist of a well-consolidated snowpack with a minimum of new snow and expected low temperatures. A warming trend or rain would make the entire Ingalls Creek drainage, as well as the ski run itself, extremely dangerous. Take ice axes and crampons.

Drive U.S. 97 to the Ingalls Creek trailhead, 7 miles south of the U.S. 2–U.S. 97 junction. Hike directly up the valley for 9.6 miles and camp near the confluence of Porcupine and Ingalls creeks in trees, well away from open slopes, at about 4100 feet. As you ski upvalley, don't tarry in the open slopes below the various gullies. The upper slopes of Porcupine Creek are concave: A release higher up could trigger slopes below.

From camp, look up toward the abrupt south ridge of Dragontail Peak. Porcupine Creek descends from the left. If conditions in the creek drainage look safe, ascend it straight on. Near 6700 feet, traverse right and up. The angle lessens above 7800 feet and soon you are at the col. You should reach it just as the sun begins to soften the snow. Descend quickly before the melting progresses too far. This is basically a 3000-foot ski run in the fall line.

The slope right of Dragontail's south buttress is a good route, too. This slope is gentler than Porcupine Creek but puts the skier onto the Enchantment Plateau, 300 feet below the summit of Dragontail. A bold tour could be made by ascending this slope, descending Asgaard Pass, climbing to Colchuck Col, and returning to Ingalls Creek. The Crystal Creek drainage is another good touring objective.

The descent along Ingalls Creek is straightforward. Wax helps to speed up the escape.

INGALLS PEAK

48

Map—
page 148

Start Point	North Fork Teanaway Road, 4240 feet
High Point	North–South Peak Col, 7320 feet
Best Time	April to June
Length	Day trip; 11 miles; 6 hours
Difficulty	Advanced; high avalanche potential
Maps	Green Trails No. 209, Mount Stuart; USGS 15-minute series, Mount Stuart

Ingalls Peak lies 2 miles west of Mount Stuart in a scenic, easily accessible area. Normally crowded in summer, the snow cover diminishes the number of visitors markedly. The open slopes above and below Ingalls Lake provide fine runs but require caution, especially when strong sun softens the snowpack.

Drive U.S. 97 (Blewett Pass Highway) to the Teanaway River road (county road No. 107, 7 miles from Interstate 90). Drive the Teanaway River road for 23 miles to the north fork of the Teanaway River (4240 feet), or as far as conditions permit.

Ingalls Peak country (Photo: Harry Hendon).

From the parking lot, hike or ski an abandoned road (Ingalls Way Trail) for 0.5 mile, then turn right up the hill, following switchbacks. In 1.6 miles (5000 feet), there is a fork in the trail. The right fork puts you at the top of Longs Pass (6300 feet) in 0.6 mile. Take the left fork, traversing northwest and climbing switchbacks for 1.6 miles to Ingalls Pass.

From Ingalls Pass, make a descending traverse, contouring left to the saddle across the valley. The saddle is reached in 1.5 miles. Drop over the saddle toward Ingalls Lake, then climb over humps on the left side to the valley east of the north and south peaks. The right side of this valley is exposed to sluffs from the south face of the north peak. Stay clear of this side. Rather, ascend the middle or left side of the valley. Do not enter this area if it is very warm. Wet-snow sluffs occur here frequently. Climb to a col at the head of the valley.

Once at the col, you may traverse south to the summit of the lesser peak, descend the northwest side (very steep), or return to Ingalls Lake to ski the slopes around and below the lake. You can also descend to Ingalls Creek. For the latter, climb to the ridge top south-southwest of Ingalls Lake, then descend southeast from near the summit of Point 7382 to regain the trail. Do not climb the north-facing slope below Longs Pass. Doing so would expose you to unknown danger from cornices far above and would give you no chance to examine the slope for stability.

Return to the car by skiing the approach route. This is a good early-season tour as possible since the south-facing slopes melt out fairly quickly.

MOUNT STUART

49

Map—
page 148

Start Point	North Fork Teanaway Road, 4240 feet
High Point	Mount Stuart False Summit, 9160 feet
Best Time	March to April
Length	Overnight; 14 miles; 10 hours
Difficulty	Advanced; high avalanche potential
Maps	Green Trails No. 209, Mount Stuart; USGS 15-minute series, Mount Stuart

Mount Stuart and its minions are visible to the north from Interstate 90 between Ellensburg and Thorp. The long snowfield descending from left to right from the false summit is the southeast shoulder. This broad slope is steep in only a few sections near the top. It is best skied in well-frozen conditions when the sun is just beginning to melt the top layer. This is a good tour because it has a reasonable and interesting approach, has good skiing (both north

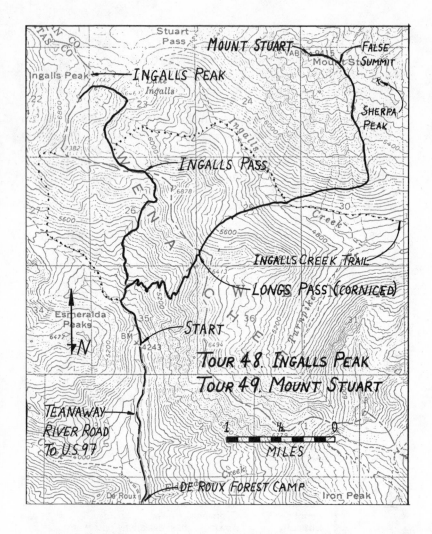

and south facing), and has spectacular views. Ice axes and crampons are suggested.

Drive to the end of the Teanaway River road, and hike the Ingalls Way Trail to Longs Pass (2.7 miles, 2000 feet elevation gain). Take a moment to examine your route and think about snow conditions. What are the current and recent temperature, precipitation, and snow conditions? What will they be higher up? Look at Stuart, especially the south rib of the false summit. The route follows the right slope of that rib all the way to the valley bottom. Memorize it and some likely looking alternatives.

Bypassing the cornices at Longs Pass may require ice axes. Descend 1200 feet to Ingalls Creek and head northeast along the forested valley floor for 0.4 mile toward the southeast shoulder of Mount Stuart. Good campsites are found in the woods along Ingalls Creek. Be sure your camp is well away from avalanche runout areas.

The southeast shoulder terminates in a broad avalanche runout area, an indicator that this tour should be attempted only in well-frozen conditions. Avoid entering Ulrichs Couloir or Cascadian Couloir, two grooves that are west of the southeast slope. These gullies are steep and narrow and, in case of slides, would act as traps. The broad southeast shoulder is a much safer route.

Ski directly up the broad avalanche slope, keeping out of the valley bottom. If there are signs of instability, or the temperature is rising, abandon the tour. Do not cross over the rib to the right, or to the left. This slope climbs 4000 feet to the false summit. The true summit lies 0.2 mile away to the west and an ice ax may be needed to reach it. Beware of cornices on the north side.

Descend the route of ascent. Once back down the valley, climb back to Longs Pass and descend to the car. If a cornice or the north slope at Longs Pass seems unstable, head upstream along Ingalls Creek for 2 miles, and gain the valley just south of Ingalls Lake. Continue southwest to Ingalls Pass, then ski back to the car. This route is only slightly longer.

SNOQUALMIE PASS, INTERSTATE 90

Besides being the primary east-west corridor through the Cascades, this highway also provides rapid access to high routes in the central Cascades and the Wenatchee Mountains.

Tours reached directly from Interstate 90 are accessible year around, but routes starting from secondary roads may not be feasible until late spring.

The Snoqualmie Pass area has a history of snow recreation dating from the 19th century, when Norwegian miners first skied the slopes behind the town of Cle Elum. This region has sufficient snow and reasonable access for ski tours from December to May. Many of the tours in the pass area depart from ski-area parking lots. During the ski season, backcountry skiers may be asked to pay a parking fee.

If the weather is particularly foul near the Cascade Crest, more benign conditions may sometimes be found near Amabilis Mountain or even farther east. A number of excellent tours can be made in the Salmon la Sac area; these tours must be timed so that road access coincides with good snow conditions.

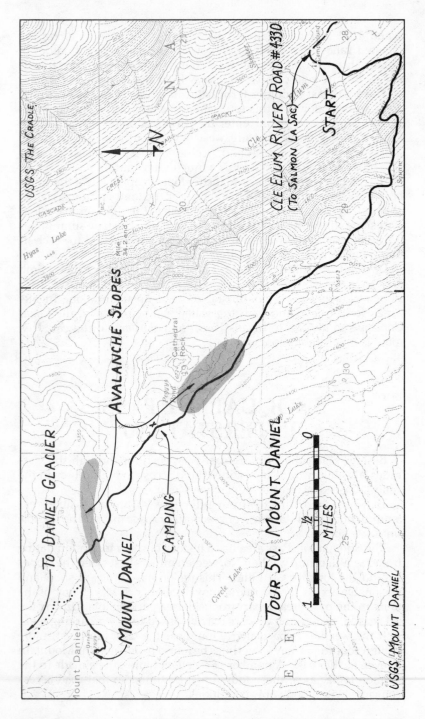

MOUNT DANIEL

50

Start Point	Cle Elum River Road, 3350 feet
High Point	Mount Daniel's East Summit, 7986 feet
Best Time	March to June
Length	Overnight; 14 miles; 8 hours
Difficulty	Advanced; glacier travel; high avalanche potential
Maps	Green Trails Nos. 176 and 208, Stevens Pass and Kachess Lake; USGS 7.5-minute series, Mount Daniel and The Cradle

Mount Daniel's massive, gently sloping shoulders support large amounts of snow ideally suited for ski touring. Its main drawback is the lack of convenient access; the Cle Elum River road is snow covered late into spring. The trick to making Daniel a successful tour is to get there just when the road melts out. An occasional obstacle blocking the last 3 miles of road is the Scatter Creek crossing, which becomes impassable when meltwater rushing across the road is too deep to drive through. Bring a tow rope in case you get stuck. This tour is a leisurely overnighter, but can be an athletic day trip. Take ice axes and crampons.

Drive Interstate 90 to the Roslyn interchange 3 miles west of Cle Elum. Drive through the town of Roslyn, past Salmon la Sac, to the road end at 3350 feet, about 33 miles from Roslyn. There is a fork 0.2 mile before the road end. Take the left spur to the trailhead. Cathedral Rock is visible to the northwest. Your objective is to reach Peggys Pond just west of the tower.

Hike the trail south and west, gaining 1000 feet in 1.8 miles. When the ridge begins to flatten, proceed northwest over rolling terrain through glades toward Cathedral Rock's south ridge. Stay above Squaw Lake. Continue for 2.5 miles, heading just left of Cathedral Rock. As you approach the mountain, the terrain forces you to move left onto a steepening hillside. Cathedral Rock now towers on the right while Deep Lake lies frozen below. Continue traversing north, climbing a few hundred feet until Peggys Pond appears in front of you (5600 feet). Camp on the snow, southwest of the lake, or on a rise to the west. This is a high-use area; stay on the snow or on trails to minimize "meadow-busting."

The route to the east summit is straightforward and evident from Peggys Pond. Head northwest to the summit visible from the lake, routefinding through cliff bands and crevasses. From the pond, climb west into a basin. In 0.3 mile the angle eases off for a bit, then steepens again to reach the Hyas Creek Glacier. The lower portion of this stagnant ice body is fairly level, and in some years a lake forms just above the glacier's terminal moraine.

The route to Mount Daniel goes directly up the center of the picture (Photo: Bryan Scott).

From the eastern end of the glacier, survey the route and pick the snow ramp that offers the easiest approach to the snowfields to the north. The headwall above the Hyas Creek Glacier can present avalanche dangers from sun-softened wet-snow slides. Plan your ascent (and descent) accordingly.

Climb the steep slope and gain the snowfield, skiing past a small spire (7700 feet). The summit lies just ahead. Approach it via the rocky ridge to the left. The gully on the east face of the summit spire has been skied, but it is known to slide. Descend to Peggys Pond via the approach.

It is easy to reach Daniel and Lynch glaciers from Peggys Pond by traversing high on the north side of Mount Daniel. (This route offers access to the middle and western summits of Mount Daniel, as well as Mount Hinman beyond.) Both glaciers are moderately steep and have extensive crevasse systems. This variation should not be attempted in unsettled weather or in conditions of limited visibility.

JOLLY MOUNTAIN

51

Start Point	Salmon la Sac, 2400 feet
High Point	Jolly Mountain, 6440 feet
Best Time	March to June, as soon as the road opens
Length	Day trip; 12 miles; 6 hours
Difficulty	Intermediate; low avalanche potential
Maps	Green Trails No. 208, Kachess Lake; USGS Kachess Lake, 15-minute series

Jolly Mountain is located northeast of Cle Elum Lake. It is not a difficult tour and affords wonderful views of the Mount Stuart and Dutch Miller Gap areas. Difficult access is the main obstacle; an ideal

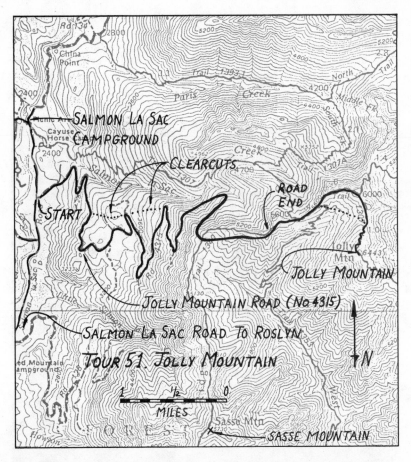

situation would be a melted-out road coupled with 12 inches of new snow higher up. The weather tends to be better here than on the west side. Plum Creek Timber Company has extended the Jolly Mountain Road (No. 4315) to within 2 miles of the summit of the peak. Public use is permitted but be alert for logging trucks. The road may be gated. Before driving past the gate, call the Forest Service to make sure it won't be locked behind you. The Forest Service can also provide information on road conditions.

Drive Interstate 90 to Exit 80 and then State Route 903 through Roslyn, past Cle Elum Lake. Little more than 1 mile before the Salmon la Sac guard station is the turnoff for the Jolly Mountain road (about 14 miles from Roslyn).

Drive the road as far as conditions permit, then ski or hike. Keep to the main road, avoiding spurs. It is possible to short-cut switchbacks near 2900 and 3500 feet, but it is hardly worth the effort. The road switchbacks up the west face of Sasse Ridge, then climbs a connecting ridge toward Jolly Mountain. Simply contour along or near the right edge of this U-curving crest toward Jolly Mountain. Fine runs can be made on gladed slopes, clear cuts, and over open heather benches. Return by retracing the approach.

Climbing Sasse Ridge to Jolly Mountain (Photo: Joe Cattellani).

AMABILIS MOUNTAIN

52

Start Point	Cabin Creek Sno-Park, 2300 feet
High Point	Amabilis Mountain, 4500 feet
Best Time	December to March
Length	Day trip; 8 miles; 4 to 6 hours
Difficulty	Intermediate; low avalanche potential
Maps	Green Trails No. 207, Snoqualmie Pass; USGS 15-minute series, Snoqualmie Pass

Amabilis Mountain offers an aerobic ascent to a broad summit with sweeping views and minor runs on both north and south slopes. This tour is best suited to Nordic equipment because of the moderate terrain. Amabilis Mountain is currently off-limits to snowmobiles. Errant snowmobilers are in violation of current USFS regulations. This is a popular area, so come early to find a place to park. A Sno-Park permit is required for this tour. They may be purchased at a Snoqualmie Summit cafe. Large amounts of new snow on the flat may indicate slab conditions at higher elevations.

Drive Interstate 90 to Exit 63, the Cabin Creek exit. Park in the

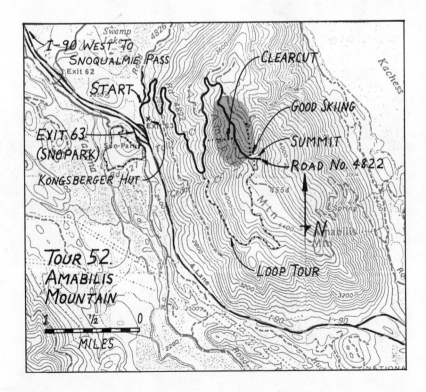

Near the top of Amabilis Mountain (Photo: Joe Cattellani).

Sno-Park area west of the highway and walk across the bridge to the Cabin Creek road. Ski the road past the Kongsberger Ski Club, a Nordic racing club, and turn right on road No. 4822, the Amabilis Mountain road. The road crosses the Kongsberger racetrack twice: Be sure to look both ways to avoid interfering with racers. Climb the road for 2 miles. At 3300 feet there is a junction. The right fork makes a loop and returns to the left fork: The round-trip distance for this tour is 8 miles from the car.

Take the left fork for better views and more interesting skiing. The clearcut on your right is cut by gullies which discharge occasional avalanches across the road so beware. Follow switchbacks to the summit ridge. Once on the broad, open plateau, ski south for 1.3 miles to the summit hump. Notice the small hanging valley on the east side of the ridge. In stable conditions this pocket sometimes affords good runs.

The descent can be made in three ways: Return over your tracks; find the southern branch of the loop and follow it to the intersection below; or ski the fall line to intersect the road below.

To find the southern end of the loop, ski south from the summit plateau, keeping out of the forest. You will cross the road in less than a mile, around 4400 feet. Follow the road to the intersection, then rejoin the crowds.

Skiing the clearcuts is an advanced tour due to routefinding, avalanche potential, and snow conditions. Before attempting this variation, you should have examined the slope on the ascent for signs of instability. To start the descent, simply head due west until the angle steepens, then pick your route. The snow here is often wind packed and crusty and conceals sharp sticks and stumps. Ski cautiously through these clearcuts.

Soft snow can sometimes be found on the lee sides of minor ridges, but be careful of slab formation. When you rejoin the road near 4000 feet, either ski the road downhill to the next clearcut or descend directly to join the road (No. 4822) near the valley bottom. Be prepared for a bushwhack if you take the latter route. The trees sometimes offer soft snow long after a snowfall.

Had enough? If not, the loop adjacent to the parking area provides a short track.

MOUNT MARGARET

53

Map—
page 158

Start Point	Gold Creek Sno-Park, 2700 feet
High Point	Mount Margaret, 5400 feet
Best Time	December to March
Length	Day trip; 9 miles; 4 to 6 hours
Difficulty	Intermediate; moderate avalanche potential
Maps	Green Trails No. 207, Snoqualmie Pass; USGS 15-minute series, Snoqualmie Pass

The huge, gleaming slope southeast of the Pacific West ski area technically belongs to Rampart Ridge. Mount Margaret lies just southeast of this hill. This tour has a flavor similar to the Amabilis tour, with the bonus of better skiing higher up. The south-facing clearcuts are best skied in late winter or early spring in low to moderate avalanche conditions. Wet-snow avalanches offer the biggest danger here. While wax makes the road ski easy, climbing skins make the ascent to the summit of Mount Margaret a delight.

Drive Interstate 90 to Exit 54, the Rocky Run exit. Drive to Gold Creek Sno-Park and continue south as far as possible. A Sno-Park permit is required. Ski the road south for 2 miles, paralleling Interstate 90 and passing some homes. When the road turns left and begins to climb, follow it for 3 miles and keep right at an intersection; 0.6 mile later, take a left fork and continue climbing for 1 mile to the Lake Lillian trailhead (3600 feet). Head northeast from the trailhead (a road peters out), climbing steeply across a branch of Wolfe Creek and up a headwall through well-spaced trees.

Soon you will come to a clearcut, bordered on the left by mature forest and on its upper edge by a saddle. Ski to the treeline and enter

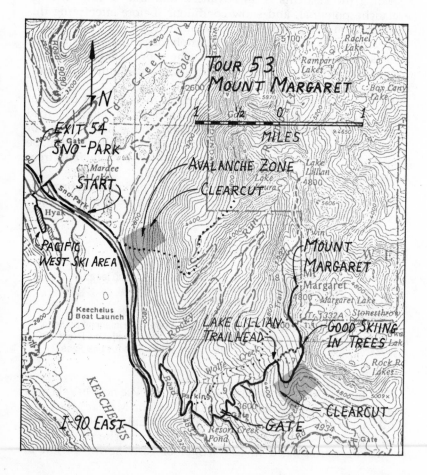

the woods near the saddle. Head north, making a climbing traverse to the false summit. The wooded true summit is a short distance away but the approach is blocked by cornices. The false summit offers a better lunch spot with better views.

Descend by heading southwest from the summit ridge. The widely spaced trees often keep powder snow long after the passage of midseason storms. It's useful to set a track so you can ski the fine powder repeatedly. To reach the clearcut western slope requires traversing cliff bands and isn't worth the effort and exposure. Ski the powder in the trees on the south side, then traverse back to the road and out to the car. If slope conditions permit, a clearcut immediately south of Wolfe Creek holds good skiing potential, giving an easy return to the road lower down. Some skiers report that ascending Mount Margaret from the slopes above Gold Creek is more direct. This route actually crosses over the southern terminus of Rampart Ridge. The western slopes are subject to sun-warmed wet-snow avalanches. Plan your trip accordingly.

Windblown snow near the summit of Amabilis Mountain, looking southwest (Photo: Joe Cattellani).

KENDALL RIDGE

54

Start Point	Gold Creek Sno-Park, 2700 feet
High Point	Kendall Ridge, 4800 feet
Best Time	January to March
Length	Day trip; 6 miles; 3 hours
Difficulty	Intermediate; moderate avalanche potential
Maps	Green Trails No. 207, Snoqualmie Pass; USGS
	15-minute series, Snoqualmie Pass

The Kendall Ridge tour ascends part of the southern flank of Kendall Peak. It is a short tour, ideal if you have only a morning but would like a little exercise and some fun skiing. Sno-Park permits are required to park at Gold Creek. Stable snow is required for the run through the clearcuts at the top.

Drive Interstate 90 to the Hyak-Rocky Run exit. Gold Creek is just east of the highway. Park and begin skiing northeast on the road. Within 0.2 mile there is a fork: Take the left road and ascend it through switchbacks to a forested section (1.5 miles). Continue skiing through woods until you approach a clearcut. The descent route passes through this clearcut.

Do not cross this open slope unless the snow is stable. If the snow

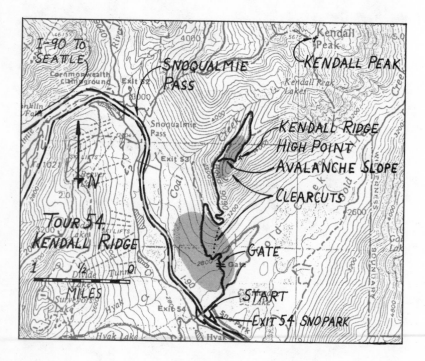

Brian Sullivan cruises Kendall Ridge powder (Photo: Kyle Klicker, Brian Sullivan).

is indeed stable, follow the curving road to the top of the clearcut. A flat logging staging area is a good place for lunch. Do not ski the northeast slope to the Gold Creek drainage. This side of Kendall Ridge is cliffy and susceptible to avalanches. Ski the clearcut on the south side of the ridge and rejoin the road used in the ascent.

Follow the logging road until you're out of the tall timber, then descend through clearcuts directly to the parking area. This is an ideal tour for very light Nordic equipment.

RED MOUNTAIN

55

Map—
page 163

Start Point	Alpental Road, 3000 feet
High Point	Red Mountain, 5890 feet
Best Time	January to April
Length	Day trip; 10 miles; 7 hours
Difficulty	Advanced; high avalanche potential
Maps	Green Trails No. 207, Snoqualmie Pass; USGS 15-minute series, Snoqualmie Pass

Red Mountain is located at the head of the upper east fork of Commonwealth Creek, 1.3 miles east of Mount Snoqualmie. This is a tour best made when the snowpack is well frozen and the sun has just melted the surface of the snow. You must leave the basin by late morning: Avalanches regularly sweep both sides of Commonwealth Basin, making this tour extremely hazardous on warm afternoons or with unsettled snow. Take ice axes and crampons.

Drive Interstate 90 to Exit 52, the Snoqualmie West exit. Park near the Commonwealth Creek trailhead just past the start of the Alpental road. Hike or ski the trail east for 0.3 mile, then follow it north along steepening terrain. The summer trail switchbacks along the

Climbing out of Commonwealth Basin (Photo: Joe Cattellani).

right side of Commonwealth Basin, but with a deep snowpack it is better to ski directly up the valley bottom.

Soon the bulk of Guye Peak will be just behind you, near 4000 feet, and you will have a clear view of the upper section of Red Mountain. As the terrain steepens, head up the creek drainage toward the Red Mountain saddle.

Near 4400 feet, begin ascending the southwest rib descending from the summit and continue following it to the top. Views of the Dutch Miller peaks and the immediate vicinity are beautiful. Descend quickly to the valley floor and ski the fall line to the Alpental road.

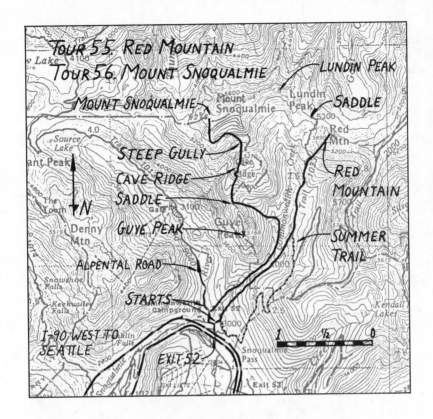

MOUNT SNOQUALMIE

56

Start Point	Alpental Road, 3000 feet
High Point	Mount Snoqualmie Summit, 6280 feet
Best Time	December to March
Length	Day trip; 4 miles; 6 hours
Difficulty	Advanced; high avalanche potential
Maps	Green Trails No. 207, Snoqualmie Pass; USGS 15-minute series, Snoqualmie Pass

This is a view tour, with a panoramic vista ranging from Mount Baker to Mount Stuart to Mount Rainier. Recoilless rifles are sometimes used to control snow buildup on Cave Ridge: Skiers are advised to check with the snow ranger before beginning a tour in this area. Take ice axes and crampons.

Leave Interstate 90 at the Alpental exit and drive a short distance up the Alpental road. Park south of the Sahale ski area (in case of crowds, park at Snoqualmie Summit and hike to the trailhead).

Climb the right side of the Sahale ski slope and continue past the tow along the right (south) shoulder of Guye Peak. In 0.7 mile, the hillside curves left (north). Contour into a streambed and climb it for 0.3 mile (elevation gain 800 feet) to the Guye-Snoqualmie saddle (about 4600 feet).

From the saddle, ski due north for 0.5 mile toward the summit of Mount Snoqualmie.

Traverse the gully leading to the southwest ridge of Snoqualmie and ascend the steep, gradually easing ridge to the summit. This ridge should not be climbed or skied except in stable conditions.

Northeast of the Guye-Snoqualmie saddle lies Cave Ridge, offering another 600 vertical feet of skiing. Avoid the steep southeastern flank of Cave Ridge. It is safer to ski the southwestern shoulder of Lundin Peak and Red Mountain to the valley floor.

The slopes of Mount Snoqualmie immediately above Alpental are too cliffy for anything but extreme skiing.

Chair Peak Basin (Photo: Brian Sullivan).

CHAIR PEAK

57

Start Point	Alpental Parking Lot, 3180 feet
High Point	Chair Peak Basin, 5600 feet
Best Time	January to May
Length	Day trip; 5 miles; 4 hours
Difficulty	Advanced; high avalanche potential
Maps	Green Trails No. 207, Snoqualmie Pass; USGS 15-minute series, Snoqualmie Pass

The Alpental basin offers short but entertaining tours with one major drawback: a high frequency of avalanches. To minimize the danger, make the tour in early season in stable conditions, that is, no warming trend and no huge dumps of new snow. Ask the snow ranger at Snoqualmie about conditions before setting out.

Drive Interstate 90 to Snoqualmie Pass, take the Alpental exit, and drive the Alpental road to the ski area parking lot. During the height of the ski season, you may be asked to pay a parking fee. To avoid a fee, park either south of the private Sahale ski area on the east side of the road, or at Snoqualmie Summit.

Ski northwest from Alpental's upper parking area up the Source Lake drainage, for 2 miles, following the Crest Trail unless snow

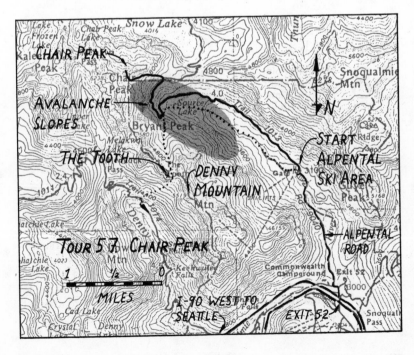

depths allow easy cross-country travel. Above Source Lake (3760 feet) climb north for 0.5 mile (4400 feet) to the basin below Chair Peak. This basin is the origin of many avalanches that fill Source Lake in the winter.

The ridge defining the north side of the basin is a good turn-around spot, with views of Mount Snoqualmie and the Dutch Miller Gap peaks. Descend by reversing the approach.

A variation of this tour can be made to Pineapple Pass, the notch just south of the Tooth. Ski up the Source Lake drainage. At the lake, climb up and south to a hanging valley above Source Lake (4800 feet). Pineapple Pass lies at the head of the valley. It is feasible to descend to Denny Creek and ski back to the summit area via the Alpental-Denny Creek road.

Other tours can be made by riding the chair lift to the top of Denny Mountain, then descending various runs to the northeast. Although they are accessible to any skier with a lift ticket, it must be emphasized that many of these runs are infrequently patrolled or controlled and should be considered backcountry tours: Take proper equipment since you're on your own.

The runs from either side of the northern spur of Denny Mountain tend to be cliffy and develop large moats in late season. If the ski patrol closes an area, the closure must be respected. In the backcountry, never ski blind. Only ski what you can see.

SILVER PEAK

58

Start Point	Pacific West Ski Resort, 2640 feet
High Point	Silver Peak, 5620 feet
Best Time	January to April
Length	Day trip; 8 miles; 6 hours
Difficulty	Advanced; moderate avalanche potential; navigation
Maps	Green Trails No. 207, Snoqualmie Pass; USGS 15-minute series, Snoqualmie Pass

Silver Peak was among the first of the Snoqualmie peaks to be climbed on skis and remains a popular objective. It is also a hazardous one, as evidenced by the periodic avalanche deaths that occur here. A scenic approach, suitable for skis, can be made from the Pacific West ski area. Wax makes the first few miles easier, while skins are better for the summit of Silver Peak. Take crampons and ice axes.

Just north (0.1 mile) of the entrance to the Pacific West parking lot is a road, normally snow covered in winter. Take this road west, contouring around the right side of the ski hill. Ski defensively to avoid being obliterated by downhill skiers. When you come to a

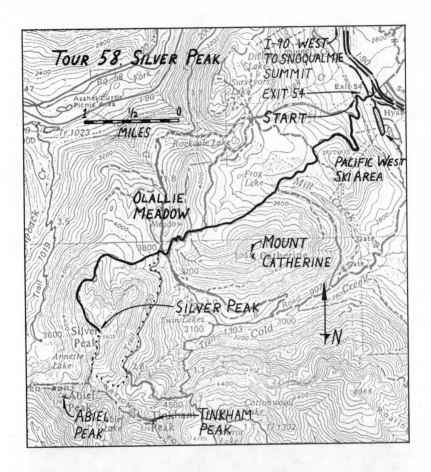

junction, take the left road. Soon you will come to another fork: Take the right one and ski southwest for 0.8 mile. When the road curves to the east, leave it and continue skiing southwest, toward Silver Peak 2.4 miles away. Ascend the gentle rise toward a saddle to Olallie Meadow beyond (3800 feet). Logging roads reach all the way to the meadow but it is faster in a heavy snowpack to ski directly to the peak than meander through the meadow.

From the meadow ski southwest to Silver Basin (1.3 miles). The north-facing basin is outlined by two ridges.

The western edge is slightly easier, but watch out for cornices. As you approach the summit, stay on or near the northwest ridge, avoiding steeper sections. Skirt these on either side, depending on conditions. Descend by retracing your approach.

The southern shoulder is also a feasible ascent route but involves traversing steeper terrain below the Silver-Tinkham saddle.

HUMPBACK MOUNTAIN

59

Start Point	Exit 47, Interstate 90, 1800 feet
High Point	Humpback Mountain, south ridge, 5170 feet
Best Time	February to March
Length	Day trip; 9 miles; 6 hours
Difficulty	Advanced; moderate avalanche potential
Maps	Green Trails Nos. 206 and 207, Bandera and
	Snoqualmie Pass; USGS 15-minute series,
	Bandera and Snoqualmie Pass

*Map—
page 170*

Humpback Mountain rises 3000 feet above the Interstate 90 corridor, but its public face doesn't display its virtue. It is the southwest

*On Granite Mountain; Humpback Mountain lies in the immediate background
(Photo: Brian Sullivan).*

shoulder that sometimes offers reasonable skiing in spring conditions. This tour must be made when the snowpack is well consolidated.

Drive Interstate 90 to Exit 47, the Granite Mountain exit, but head for the south side of the highway. Drive the south-heading access road for 0.2 mile, and park. Take the right road at the T, and follow it for 1.4 miles to a junction. Take the left fork and begin contouring left around Humpback Mountain. In 0.7 mile you are in the Hansen Creek drainage. Pass under an old railroad bridge and continue heading south as the road makes a left, then a right switchback. When the road approaches Hansen Creek, leave it at any convenient place (avalanche path near 2900 feet) and begin climbing up through slide alder, trees, and cliff bands. Continue climbing southeast, heading for the ridge crest at 4600 feet. Watch out for cornices on the east side. Climb the crest north to the summit if conditions and time allow.

Descend by retracing your tracks. Do not return so late in the day that the snowpack is sodden and unstable.

The hillsides across Hansen Creek are inviting too but present a lesser challenge for skiers. They are, however, better anchored (they are clearcuts) and offer an alternative objective in case conditions appear unsafe on Humpback. For either tour, take a small wax kit for the long, nearly level return.

GRANITE MOUNTAIN

60

Start Point	Exit 47, Interstate 90, 1800 feet
High Point	Granite Mountain, 5600 feet
Best Time	February to April
Length	Day trip; 8 miles; 6 hours
Difficulty	Advanced; low avalanche potential
Maps	Green Trails No. 207, Snoqualmie Pass; USGS 15-minute series, Snoqualmie Pass

Map— page 170

Granite Mountain is that gleaming bulk across Interstate 90 from Humpback Mountain. In early spring, once the snowpack is well consolidated, this is a worthwhile ski tour, both because of its position and the long runs it offers. Sometimes powder or surface-hoar snow is found on Granite's northern faces. Stay out of the huge gullies that furrow the southern slope; the ridges usually offer better skiing and are safer.

Drive Interstate 90 to Exit 47 and park at the trailhead parking lot north of the highway. Follow the trail as it switchbacks east and west to 2250 feet, then begin a climbing traverse heading generally northeast, staying on the broad ridge west of the major avalanche-gully

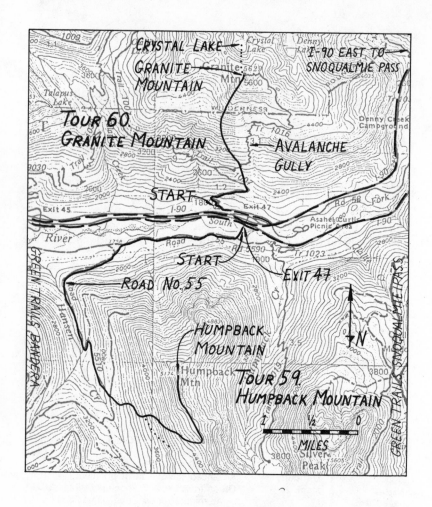

system. Make every effort to stay out of the numerous gullies that divide the south face. If there is deep snow, abandon the tour. If the snow is frozen hard, consider the situation. There may be powder on the north side but not if recent freezing levels were much higher than 4000 feet with any precipitation.

If conditions warrant, head generally northwest toward the southwest ridge (4000 feet), then climb it toward the summit.

Runs can be made toward Crystal and Denny lakes or down the broad and often corn-snow-graced southwest ridge. Avoid cornices and windslab on some of the northern slopes.

Descend with enough time to reach the car by dark. Use the route of ascent.

MOUNT RAINIER AND AREAS SOUTH

The southern Cascades, with the exception of the volcanoes, lack the rugged alpine aspect of the northern range. Nevertheless, challenging tours abound. Temperatures are generally a few degrees higher. In compensation, many of the tours take place at higher elevations.

Van Trump Park on Mount Rainier's west side (Photo: Joe Cattellani).

This section covers three general areas: the area accessible from the north side of Mount Rainier, via State Route 410; the area accessible from the west and south sides of Mount Rainier National Park, via State Routes 165 and 7; finally, the area south of the park. The USGS Mount Rainier National Park map (1:50,000 scale) is used for many of the tours in and around the park.

State Route 410 leads to the Crystal Mountain ski area, the White River entrance to the park, and to the Chinook-Cayuse Pass area. Chinook Pass is closed fairly early in the season but Cayuse stays open a few weeks longer. When both passes are finally closed for the winter, the highway is gated at the Crystal Mountain turnoff. This unfortunate policy turns midwinter day tours into major expeditions.

There are large elk herds in this area. It is sometimes possible to see these magnificent animals grazing along the banks of the White River.

NORSE PEAK

61

Start Point	Crystal Mountain Ski Area, 4400 feet
High Point	Norse Peak, 6860 feet
Best Time	January to April
Length	Day trip; 7 miles; 6 hours
Difficulty	Intermediate; moderate avalanche potential
Maps	Green Trails No. 271, Bumping Lake; USGS 15-minute series, Bumping Lake

Crystal Mountain's skiing potential is largely undeveloped. It is necessary to go touring to fully appreciate the abundant resource that is available here. One of the better tours in the valley is the backside of Norse Peak, the mountain on your left as you enter the skiing complex. The upper slopes of the north side of Norse Peak often have powder weeks after a storm, while there is good skiing on sheltered slopes of Bullion Basin even during storms.

Drive State Route 410 to the Crystal Mountain road. Take this road to the ski area, parking east of the road just below the abandoned Bullion Basin ski run. The lifts are gone now, but logged ski runs are still apparent. Ski directly up the hill, coming to a road in 0.2 mile (300 feet elevation gain). Take this road right, then left at a fork. In 0.1 mile is a switchback. Take it and, immediately after the turn, begin heading north on an abandoned jeep trail. This trail crosses Bullion Creek at 4900 feet, then begins to switchback up the hill on the north side of the drainage. The slope above here is prone to slide.

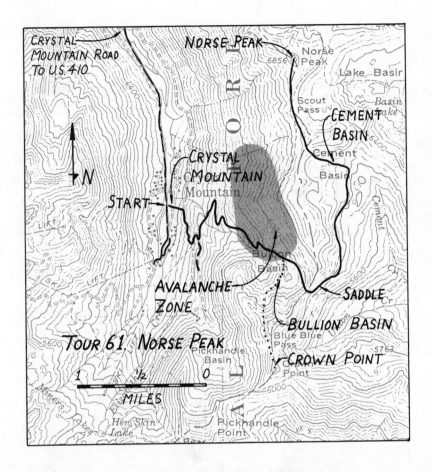

Contour to the southeast for 2 miles (keep well above the lake), skiing along the open slope. Climb to the saddle (6200 feet) southeast of the lake. To ski Union or Cement basins, descend the steep east side of the 6200-foot pass, heading north-northeast. As soon as the angle eases somewhat, descend to Union Basin, or continue north to Cement Basin. The skiing here is steep, primarily in gladed woods. If you wish to climb Norse Peak, head north to Cement Basin and regain the ridge to the west as soon as practical. Cornices may prevent this until you are 1.8 miles north of the 6200-foot pass. From here, ski the ridge north to Norse Peak (2.8 miles north of Bullion Basin).

Later in spring, when the snowpack has strengthened, it may be safe to descend directly from the summit of Norse Peak to the ski area. It is steep and should not be attempted in early season since this area slides often, and in large sections.

Otherwise, return by skiing down Bullion Basin and out to the car. For a very brief tour, with good views, head up to Bullion Basin but ascend the ridge running south to Crown Point (about 6500 feet).

SILVER BASIN

62

Start Point	Crystal Mountain Ski Area, 4400 feet
High Point	Silver King, 7000 feet
Best Time	November to April
Length	Day trip; 4 miles; 5 hours
Difficulty	Intermediate; moderate avalanche potential
Maps	Green Trails Nos. 270 and 271, Bumping Lake and Mount Rainier East; USGS 15-minute series, Bumping Lake and Mount Rainier East

Directly south of the Crystal Mountain ski area are three basins: Silver, Campbell, and Crystal. Slopes above these basins provide

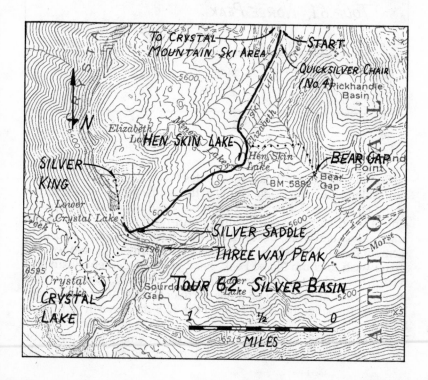

Deep powder in Silver Basin (Photo: Gary Brill).

fine skiing, especially in early season when the snow on lower slopes is heavy. Overnight tours are feasible, with safe campsites available in all three basins. If you do plan an overnight tour, park in the designated overnight area. Sign in with the ski patrol for all back-country tours and be sure to inquire about avalanche hazards.

From Enumclaw, drive State Route 410 to the Crystal Mountain ski area. Take chair lift No. 4 (Quicksilver) or ski up the hill, staying well off the runs. At the head of the lift continue south to Silver Basin past Hen Skin and Miners lakes. If the snow is stable, turn west 0.5 mile past the lakes and ascend to Silver Saddle or Silver King. Good runs can be made from these slopes in stable conditions.

From the saddle, it is possible to descend the far side to Crystal Lake, then return by climbing back up. Another side trip can be made to Bear Gap (see the next tour). *Sign out* with the ski patrol when you return to the ski area.

CHINOOK PASS

63

Start Point	Chinook Pass, 5440 feet
High Point	Yakima Peak, 6230 feet; or Naches Peak, 6460 feet
Best Time	November
Length	Day trip; 4 miles; 4 hours
Difficulty	Intermediate; high avalanche potential
Maps	Green Trails No. 270, Mount Rainier East; USGS 15-minute series, Mount Rainier National Park

Map—
page 178

The Chinook-Cayuse Pass area provides short tours that are at once accessible and reasonably safe.

Drive State Route 410 east from Enumclaw over Cayuse Pass to Chinook Pass. From Chinook it is possible to make tours around Naches and Yakima peaks. If you are in a traveling mood, park your car at Tipsoo Lakes, then ski southeast along the highway for 0.1 mile to the trailhead on the south side of the highway. Make a counterclockwise climbing traverse around Naches Peak to the notch above the bowl on the eastern side. Expect avalanche conditions near the crest of the bowl if strong winds have accompanied any snowfall. Complete the circuit by traversing low on the north side, to avoid cliffs higher up, and returning to State Route 410 at the pass. From the pass, you may cross the highway and ski southeast through woods for 0.1 mile to reach your car or ascend the northwest shoulder of Naches for some fall line skiing.

The northwest shoulder of Naches is divided by glades that are sheltered from the wind and sun and often hold powder for days. It's a worthwhile afternoon just to ski these runs repeatedly.

Yakima Peak also offers excellent runs through treeless belts. The south face has rock slides and heather slopes that require little snow to make them skiable runs. Kneepads are strongly suggested. If you are interested in climbing these two mountains, take note: Both summits require ice axes and possibly a rope for safe winter ascents.

If Chinook Pass is closed, park at Cayuse Pass and take the valley shortcuts to Chinook Pass. Return via the same route. Do not follow the highway from Cayuse Pass since it is exposed to high avalanche danger.

The forested western slope of Yakima Peak is broken by glades (Photo: Harry Hendon).

CHINOOK PASS TO CRYSTAL MOUNTAIN TRAVERSE

64

Map — page 178

Start Point	Chinook Pass, 5450 feet; or Cayuse Pass, 4700 feet
High Point	Sourdough Gap, 6500 feet
Best Time	November; April
Length	Day trip; 12 miles; 9 hours
Difficulty	Advanced; high avalanche potential; navigation
Maps	Green Trails Nos. 270 and 271, Mount Rainier and Bumping Lake; USGS 15-minute series, Mount Rainier and Bumping Lake

This challenging tour takes the skier to seldom-traveled (in winter) terrain with challenging skiing. The route travels just east of the Cascade Crest along the Crest Trail between Cayuse Pass and the Crystal Mountain ski area. Stable snow conditions are required for this tour; windslab can form in many locations on this above-

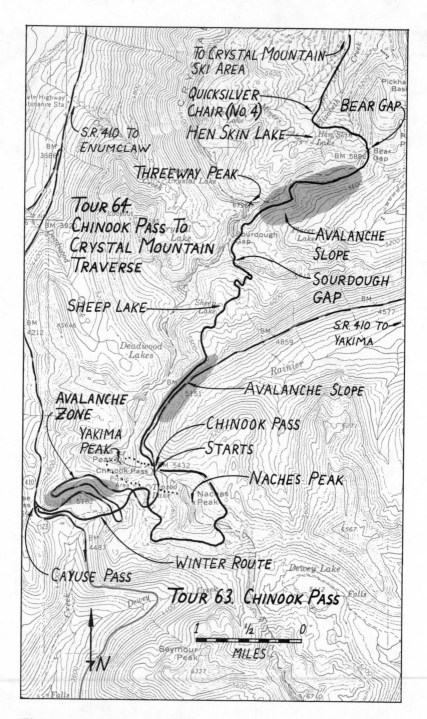

To Crystal Mountain Ski Area

Quicksilver Chair (No. 4)

Bear Gap

S.R. 410 to Enumclaw

Hen Skin Lake

Threeway Peak

Tour 64. Chinook Pass To Crystal Mountain Traverse

Avalanche Slope

Sourdough Gap

Sheep Lake

S.R. 410 to Yakima

Avalanche Slope

Avalanche Zone

Chinook Pass

Yakima Peak

Starts

Naches Peak

Winter Route

Cayuse Pass

Tour 63. Chinook Pass

1   ½   0

MILES

N

timberline tour. Be especially wary of the area between Sourdough and Bear gaps.

Begin from either Cayuse Pass or Chinook Pass. If you start at Cayuse, ski east past Tipsoo Lakes to Chinook Pass (see Tour 63). Ski north from Chinook Pass (5450 feet) toward a patch of timber, making a rising traverse above State Route 410. The slopes above the road are avalanche prone.

Pass the timber on the west side, still heading north, and ascend that basin that holds Sheep Lake (5800 feet). Northeast of the basin lies Sourdough Gap (6500 feet, 3.5 miles from Chinook Pass), the first pass of the traverse. (Sourdough Gap is not correctly identified on either Green Trails or USGS maps.)

From Sourdough Gap you can see Placer Lake below and to the east. The route turns northeast, descending steep and corniced slopes for 600 feet. Continue skiing east on a level traverse above the Morse Creek basin. In 2 miles you should reach Bear Gap (5882 feet). Just before the gap is a small bowl. Cross this slope high rather than low, and ski through Bear Gap. Once over the pass, head northwest for 0.8 mile to the top of the Quicksilver chair lift (No. 4). Ski the hill and meet your friends below.

Stable snow conditions are required for this route. After the road to Cayuse Pass is blocked, it becomes more feasible to do this tour in reverse. Be sure to take the road shortcuts above Cayuse Pass and be prepared for a 6-mile road ski, much of it downhill (take kicker wax). Arrange for a ride at the junction of State Route 410 and the Crystal Mountain access road. The road ski out is exposed to avalanche danger from a number of gullies that intersect the road.

SUMMERLAND

65		
	Start Point	Fryingpan Creek, 3900 feet
	High Point	Summerland, 5440 feet; Fryingpan Glacier, 8600 feet; or Little Tahoma, 11,120 feet
	Best Time	October to November; March to June
	Length	Day trip to Summerland; 9 miles; 6 to 10 hours
	Difficulty	Advanced; high avalanche potential; navigation; glacier skiing above Summerland
Map— page 183	**Maps**	USGS 7.5-minute series, Mount Rainier East; USGS 15-minute series, Mount Rainier

A sense of remoteness, 2000-foot runs, and better-than-average weather characterize the Summerland tour. This and other above-timberline tours in the park should not be attempted in any but stable weather conditions. Ice axes and crampons are suggested for this tour.

Enter Mount Rainier National Park via the White River entrance, stopping to inquire about snow and weather conditions. The Summerland trail starts on the west side of Fryingpan Creek, about 4 miles past the White River entrance ranger station. The first 2 miles climb gently to the southwest on a broad, marked path through mature timber. At 2 miles (4500 feet), switchbacks climb steeply above the Fryingpan Creek canyon then continue due west up the Fryingpan drainage. Do not enter the open valley if you suspect avalanche danger! Under stable conditions, follow the main stream branch (right) to an open bowl beneath Fryingpan Glacier.

From here you can see a small knoll (6000 feet) to the south. Head south toward this bump. A stone shelter lies 0.1 mile to the southwest of the knoll but is frequently filled with drifted snow. Bring a tent if you plan to spend the night.

Fryingpan Glacier, southwest of Summerland, offers excellent skiing. To reach the Fryingpan Glacier climb directly up steep snow or rock just west of Meany Crest, then continue climbing southwest past Point 7573. The glacier is least crevassed along its eastern edge. For information on climbing Little Tahoma, see Fred Beckey's *Cascade Alpine Guide*, Volume 1. The small glaciers (6400-7400 feet) 0.8 mile

Meany Crest, Little Tahoma and Mount Rainier (Photo: Brian Sullivan).

south of the shelter provide a closer destination. Good early-season skiing can often be found on old névé covered with fresh snow.

Above 6500 feet, avalanche potential increases for most any destination in this area. Also, steep slopes make it important to carry ice axes and crampons above this elevation.

Return by reversing the approach.

INTERGLACIER

66

Map—
page 183

Start Point	White River Campground, 4400 feet
High Point	Steamboat Prow, 9700 feet
Best Time	May to June
Length	Day trip; 12 miles; 8 hours
Difficulty	Advanced; glacier skiing; high avalanche potential
Maps	USGS 7.5-minute series, Sunrise and Mount Rainier East

The Sunrise side of Rainier has slightly less mean annual precipitation, more difficult access, and about the same spectacular scenery and skiing as the southwest shoulder. This area is in the rain shadow of the volcano and exhibits significantly different vegetation patterns than the wetter west side. It is not easily approachable in early spring, but fine day tours can be made as soon as the Sunrise road is open.

Drive State Route 410 to the White River entrance and ask if the White River ranger station is open. If not, make your inquiries about recent snowfall, wind, and temperature here. It is not sufficient to simply ask about avalanche danger. Use Park Service information, but make your own ongoing evaluations as you travel: An overall avalanche hazard evaluation is generally meaningless when 4000 vertical feet of terrain are involved. For example, the slopes were stable (frozen solid, in fact) on the Interglacier after a rainstorm dumped 2 inches of rain in June 1985. Higher up, that precipitation fell as snow, which avalanched and injured two climbers. A proper review of earlier weather patterns would have informed the climbers that high winds were associated with the storm and that huge slab formation could be expected. In fact, that's what happened. Slabs released all around the mountain for weeks after that storm.

Continue to the White River campground (4400 feet) or as close as snow permits. If you end up skiing the Sunrise highway, turn left on the White River road, just after the White River bridge. Total distance from State Route 410 to the campground is about 6.5 miles.

The trail leaves the west end of the campground and follows the right side of the White River, climbing gradually for 3 miles. A steeper section is climbed in two switchbacks and Glacier Basin is gained in another 0.5 mile. There are campsites here (about 6000 feet).

Continue upvalley west of the glacier until it becomes possible to traverse to the middle of the Interglacier. Crevasses near 7800 feet mark the head of the initial steep section. Pass these on your right, close to cliff bands. Not too close. Rockfall and snow sluff often descend on the route from above. It is useful to mark the uphill side

The Interglacier is the diamond-shaped ice body in right center (Photo: Austin Post, USGS).

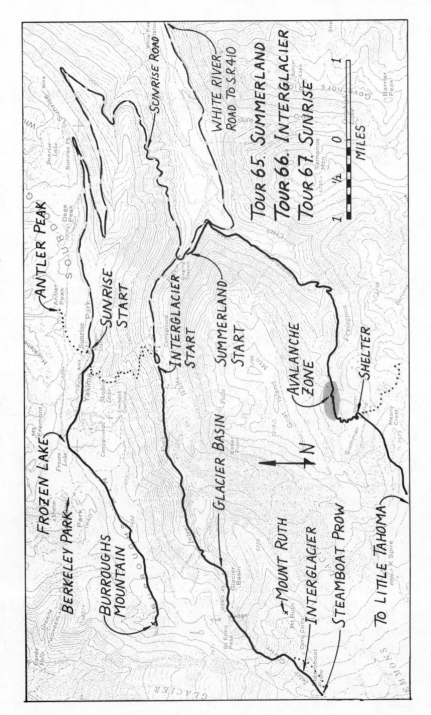

TOUR 65. SUMMERLAND

TOUR 66. INTERGLACIER

TOUR 67. SUNRISE

WHITE RIVER
ROAD TO S.R.410

SUNRISE ROAD

ANTLER PEAK

SUNRISE START

INTERGLACIER START

SUMMERLAND START

AVALANCHE ZONE

SHELTER

FROZEN LAKE

BERKELEY PARK

BURROUGHS MOUNTAIN

GLACIER BASIN

MOUNT RUTH

INTERGLACIER

STEAMBOAT PROW

TO LITTLE TAHOMA

N

MILES

of unobvious crevasse crossings with wands. Ascend the next 500 feet, crossing another crevasse band at 8800 feet to the more gently sloping glacier above. From here, ski directly toward the high point on the ridge above, or ski slightly east to the ridge and follow it to the high point of Steamboat Prow. The nearly level area east of the Prow (8600 feet), but still on the crest, is called Camp Curtis.

To descend, simply ski the route of ascent: a 4000-foot run down the Interglacier. If the glacier is too crevassed or icy, the slopes on the north side of Mount Ruth may have snow suitable for skiing.

SUNRISE

67

Map—
page 183

Start Point	Sunrise Parking Lot, 6400 feet
High Point	Burroughs Mountain, 7830 feet
Best Time	November; May to June
Length	Day trip; 8 miles; 5 hours
Difficulty	Intermediate; moderate avalanche potential
Maps	USGS 7.5-minute series, Mount Rainier East and White River Park; 1:50,000, Mount Rainier National Park

Sunrise Park is slightly removed from the mountain and has better views (not to mention better weather) because of it. The key to a successful tour here is either arriving right after a cold storm or waiting until the snow has turned to corn snow. This route is best suited to Nordic equipment. Car camping is not permitted but there is a walk-in camp a short distance from the parking lot.

Find the access road to the walk-in campground. It begins near the west end of the parking lot on the south side. In 0.7 mile the road turns southwest, just past a streambed descending from Frozen Lake. Leave the road and head uphill, keeping just right of a gentle ridge. The slope quickly becomes steeper. Climb 300 feet to the Frozen Lake basin, then turn left and begin skiing west along Burroughs Mountain. Make a climbing traverse, crossing a steep section to the false summit of Burroughs. This area has near-tundra vegetation that's both beautiful and fragile: Stay on the snow and on the trails. Continue heading southwest to the summit of Burroughs. Return by retracing the route of ascent or descending directly north and contouring near the 6400-foot level back to Frozen Lake.

The small pocket glacier on the north slope of Burroughs is steep but has been skied. More gentle terrain in Berkeley Park may hold more appeal for intermediate skiers.

In very early season the slopes just north of the parking lot may be snow covered. Point 6951 and Antler Peak (7020 feet) are good objectives when the snow surface is just beginning to thaw.

CARBON GLACIER

68

Start Point	Ipsut Creek Campground, 2460 feet
High Point	Carbon Glacier, 8000 feet
Best Time	April to June
Length	Day trip; 10 miles; 12 hours
Difficulty	Intermediate; glacier skiing; high avalanche potential
Maps	USGS 7.5-minute series, Mowich Lake; USGS 15-minute series, Mount Rainier National Park

Map— page 186

This is a view tour, well suited to Nordic skis. A moderately long approach up a gentle, broad glacier puts the skier right into the hall of the Mountain King. This is a better overnight tour than a day trip; with more time skiers can approach the north wall more closely (not too closely).

Drive State Route 165 from Buckley to the Carbon River bridge and beyond to the Carbon River entrance of the park. Drive as far as

Low down on the Carbon Glacier (Photo: Gary Brill).

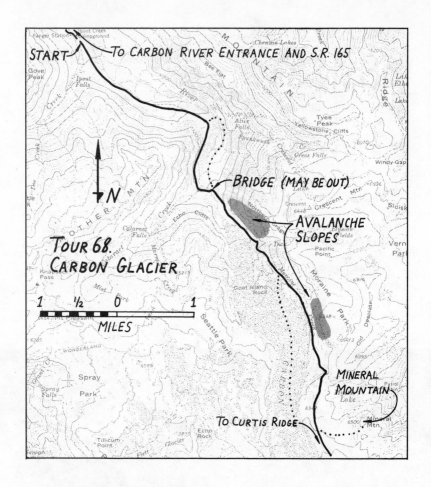

START — To CARBON RIVER ENTRANCE AND S.R. 165

BRIDGE (MAY BE OUT)

AVALANCHE SLOPES

TOUR 68.
CARBON GLACIER

1   ½   0   1
MILES

MINERAL MOUNTAIN

TO CURTIS RIDGE

conditions permit (the road may be gated before the Ipsut Creek campground); call the Park Service in advance, both regarding the gate and the state of the Carbon River bridge (see below). The trail l3aves the campground at its upstream end. Hike through woods along the Carbon River until you come out of the woods along the river. Cross the stream where convenient. There is a bridge at 2840 feet and another at 3440 feet, just below the Carbon Glacier snout, but these may be closed for the winter season. If the bridges are not up, crossing the river may be extremely difficult and dangerous.

The river is typically low in winter and may be crossed near 3000 feet by boulder hopping. (Use the open bridges during spring runoff.) Continue up the east bank to the narrow gorge that confines the glacier's snout. Scurry under the Northern Crags (watch out for rockfall and sluffs) and make the steep traverse above the glacier, gaining elevation steadily.

If the glacier looks well covered with snow, consider descending and skiing directly up it, to the right of Goat Island Rock. Ropes and other glacier-travel impedimenta are advised for going up this crevassed portion. Otherwise, continue up the trail, crossing Dick Creek and skirting the lateral moraine on its left side. Cross over the moraine and gain the glacier 1.5 miles from its snout, near 5500 feet. The glacier slopes very gently here and routefinding is straightforward. Continue heading upglacier for 2 miles until you come to a steep, broken section near 6800 feet. Pass this on the right, then turn southeast toward Curtis Ridge. The glacier steepens and is more broken here. Ski along the lower slopes of the ridge to make an end run around crevasses near 8000 feet, then traverse right to the base of Liberty Ridge and high camp. Do not camp too close to the wall, which is subject to occasional massive avalanches.

Descend by retracing your approach. An alternative tour is to not ski the glacier but to follow the snow-covered trail to Mystic Lake or Curtis Ridge. Mystic Lake lies between Old Desolate and Mineral Mountain and is 12 miles from Ipsut Creek. Curtis Ridge is reached from the basin below the Mystic Lake saddle (6000 feet). Ski due south, routefinding through steep sections above 6400 feet. Once this cliffy section is passed, the gentler east shoulder of Curtis Ridge provides few obstacles to 8000 feet. Descend by heading directly toward Mineral Mountain, then traversing around it to the southwest. Complete the descent by retracing the approach.

RUSSELL GLACIER

69

Start Point	Mowich Lake Parking Lot, 4980 feet
High Point	Observation Rock, 8360 feet
Best Time	October to November; May to July
Length	Day trip; 10 miles; 12 hours
Difficulty	Intermediate; navigation; high avalanche potential
Maps	USGS 7.5-minute series, Mowich Lake; USGS 15-minute series, Mount Rainier National Park

Map— page 188

This tour provides intermediate skiing amid the primordial splendor of the Nordwand of Mount Rainier, with minimal crevasse problems. As an early-season tour it is feasible only if the road to Mowich Lake is still open or your party is equipped with a snowmobile. Otherwise, the long road approach would require an after-dark exit. It is possible to enter this area from the Carbon River

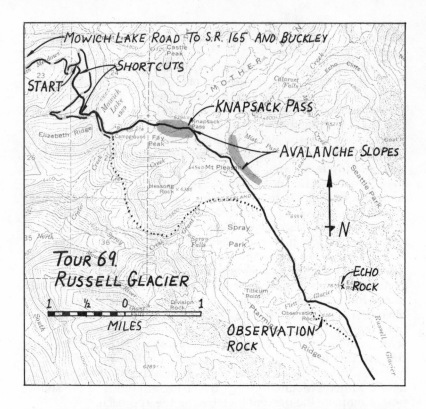

entrance (Tour 68) via the Marmot Creek trail and Seattle Park. Nevertheless, the isolation, grandeur, and ski runs of this area make the tour worthwhile.

Drive State Route 165 from Buckley to the Carbon River bridge and beyond to a junction. Take the right fork to the Mowich Lake entrance of Mount Rainier National Park. There is a gate at the park boundary but this is often open. Call park headquarters at Longmire to make certain it is. The road to Mowich Lake is 11 miles long and is frequently snow covered for miles. In that case, ski the road.

About 3 miles from the gate is the first of 2 shortcuts (no snow machines!) which save a few miles of road skiing. It heads southwest along the left of a creek (4360 feet). Follow the red metal flags which mark the trail. The trail crosses the road as it completes a curve. The second shortcut begins directly across the road from the end of the first.

When the second section of trail rejoins the road, follow it left to Mowich Lake and the ranger station situated on the southeast shore.

Ascend the left (north) side of the steep hill behind the ranger station for 500 feet and continue into the open basin north of Fay Peak. This basin leads east to Knapsack Pass. Abandon the tour before entering the basin if you suspect avalanche danger. Otherwise, ascend the steep headwall of the basin to Knapsack Pass.

From Knapsack Pass (6200 feet) make a descending traverse to the right (southeast), contouring below the slopes of Mount Pleasant to about 5600 feet. Beware of perched cornices on the cliffs above! Now climb the undulating slopes of Spray Park for about 2.5 miles (southeast). Observation Rock (8360 feet), a prominent rocky point, becomes visible to the right of Echo Rock (7870 feet). These landmarks are visible from Seattle on clear days.

The Flett Glacier (directly below Observation Rock) is mildly crevassed. Avoid the very steep upper sections by traversing left, then heading right (south) again to climb Observation Rock.

Descend to the Russell Glacier via a notch on the north side of Observation Rock. This glacier offers long runs on relatively gentle slopes to about 9200 feet. There is little danger of avalanches from Liberty Wall. Overall, the Russell Glacier becomes increasingly crevassed toward its confluence with the Carbon Glacier.

An alternative approach (or exit) can be made via the trail heading south from Mowich Lake. This trail is about 1 mile longer but avoids the steep climb over Knapsack Pass.

Make certain that you are at the road by dark: Descending the steeper trail sections can be extremely unpleasant.

Echo and Observation rocks from Spray Park (Photo: Gary Brill).

PUYALLUP CLEAVER

70

Start Point	West Side Road, 4000 feet
High Point	Puyallup Cleaver, 9200 feet
Best Time	May to July
Length	Overnight; 11 miles; 9 to 12 hours
Difficulty	Advanced; glacier travel; high avalanche potential
Maps	USGS 7.5-minute series, Mount Rainier West and Mount Wow; USGS 15-minute series, Mount Rainier National Park

Puyallup Cleaver divides the Puyallup Glacier from the Tahoma Glacier. This route brings the skier high on the mountain with minimal glacier travel. Few people climb this side of Rainier. It is a fairly solitary route, frequented by mountain goats.

Drive State Route 706 to the Nisqually entrance of Mount Rainier National Park. Take the West Side Road, 1 mile past the entrance, to the Klapatche Park trailhead (11.5 miles from the junction, 3700 feet). Hike and ski the trail to Klapatche Park (2.5 miles, 5500 feet) and continue east to Saint Andrews Park (0.7 mile). Take a minute to evaluate avalanche conditions before crossing the steep slopes below Aurora Peak. Their southern exposure and steep, grassy surface become extremely dangerous slide areas with warm weather and a sodden snowpack.

From Saint Andrews Lake, head east up the valley to Tokaloo Spire (1.3 miles, 7680 feet). Good bivouac sites are found on benches south of the spire.

Climb along the ridge uphill of the spire and contour onto the edge of the Puyallup Glacier on the north side of the Puyallup Cleaver, near 8000 feet, when it becomes feasible to do so. Continue with a climbing traverse over steep subridges that connect to the

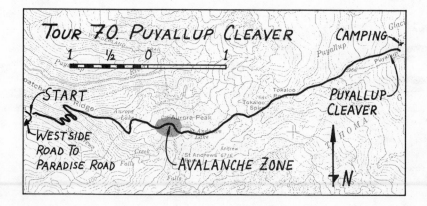

The Puyallup Cleaver route meanders from lower right to center (Photo: Austin Post, USGS).

cleaver at right angles, and angle around a large buttress to a saddle at 9200 feet. This is the classic high camp for summit attempts of this route and should be considered the high point of a day trip. Descend quickly, following your tracks back to Saint Andrews Park. Before crossing the slopes below Aurora Peak, look for signs of sun-caused instability, such as sluffs or donuts. If you suspect any, wait until the shadows have a chance to freeze the snowpack, and hike out by headlamp. The trail is well maintained.

VAN TRUMP PARK

71

Map — page 193

Start Point	Christine Falls, 3670 feet; or Nisqually Bridge, 4000 feet
High Point	Van Trump Glaciers, 9500 feet
Best Time	January to April
Length	Day trip; 8 miles; 8 hours
Difficulty	Advanced; glacier skiing; high avalanche potential
Map	USGS 7.5-minute series, Mount Rainier West

The Van Trump Park tour is a fine alternative to "Oh, No! Not Muir again!" Its remoteness and good skiing give the tour a distinctly

Van Trump Park (Photo: Brian Sullivan).

different flavor from the carnival of Paradise (see Tour 73), with minimal glacier skiing. Snow stability must be considered before setting out; ask the ranger.

Enter the park via the Paradise highway and drive to the Christine Falls trailhead, about 3 miles above Longmire. The trail crosses Van Trump Creek 0.3 mile above the road and continues up the right side of the creek. From here to Comet Falls (another mile), the trail contours along a steep hillside, with considerable avalanche hazard. Be certain that conditions are stable before setting out. Even then, listen and look for warning signs and turn back if they exist.

About 200 yards below the falls, ascend a steep hillside to the right (east) of the falls for 700 feet to Van Trump Park where a spectacular vista awaits.

Good skiing is possible all the way to 10,000 feet. This side of the mountain is generally more sheltered from the wind than the Muir Snowfield. Consequently, the snow tends to be smoother. On the descent, be sure not to stray west into the Kautz Creek drainage.

When there is a deep snowpack, the regular route can be bypassed by skiing northwest from Christine Falls for 0.5 mile, gaining 1000 feet in the process. At about 4500 feet, begin skiing due north until,

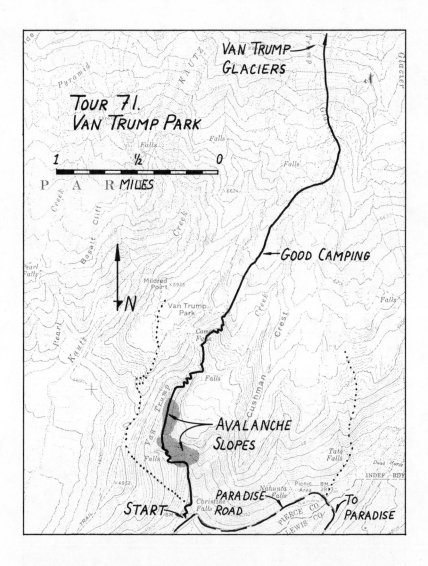

TOUR 71.
VAN TRUMP PARK

VAN TRUMP
GLACIERS

GOOD CAMPING

AVALANCHE
SLOPES

START   PARADISE
        ROAD

TO
PARADISE

in 1 mile, the plateau is gained. The ascent is steep but is not as exposed to avalanches as the first approach.

A third alternative is possible. This approach requires climbing the hill above the west (left) side of the Nisqually Glacier snout. Leave the car at the Nisqually River bridge, and ascend the open and partly wooded slopes for 1 mile and 2000 feet. Here you can head northwest to Van Trump Park. This route offers a descent that is more suitable for skiing than the others. Finding the descent, however, is sometimes tricky. Wands help here.

TATOOSH RANGE

72

Start Point	Narada Falls Parking Lot, 4570 feet
High Point	Castle-Unicorn Saddle, 6200 feet
Best Time	December to May
Length	Day trip; 4 miles; 6 to 8 hours
Difficulty	Intermediate; high avalanche potential
Maps	USGS 7.5-minute series, Mount Rainier East and Packwood

This tour provides access to the north and south slopes of the Tatoosh Range. Some of the best skiing in the park is found below the notch between The Castle and Unicorn peaks.

From the Nisqually entrance of Rainier National Park, follow the Paradise road to Longmire. During and usually after storms, the highway is sometimes blocked here, so it is worth calling ahead to learn the conditions. Follow the highway to the Narada Falls viewpoint and park. Water and heated rest rooms are available.

If the open slopes above the east end of the parking lot are "Closed to Skiers" (Park Service sign), hike 0.3 mile up the road to the junction of Stevens Canyon and then 0.2 mile along the latter to another intersection. Leave the road here and climb southeast over a 5150-foot pass to Reflection Lakes. Otherwise, ski the hill behind the

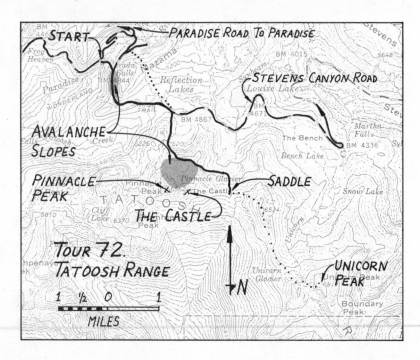

Descending the north side of the Unicorn-Castle saddle (Photo: Harry Hendon).

comfort station up to the Stevens Canyon road. Either way, ski the gentle downhill grade to Reflection Lakes basin for 1.5 miles, past a stream descending to Reflection Lakes.

Looking directly south to the peaks of the Tatoosh Range, you will see pointed Pinnacle Peak and, farther left, an obvious Castle and distant (southeast) Unicorn Peak. It is imperative to avoid the steep slopes below Pinnacle Peak: From the road, make a climbing traverse southeast to the tree-covered ridge running northwest from Castle-Pinnacle. Climb this ridge, keeping away from steep slopes on either side of the ridge near 5400 feet. Continue up a moderately steep bowl to the saddle between Unicorn Peak and The Castle (cornices likely).

From the saddle, runs on both sides of the ridge are possible, keeping avalanche hazard in mind. By traversing left from the saddle you can climb to the summit of Unicorn Peak. The southwest slope of Unicorn offers runs 3000 feet long. The north slope of the saddle has cliff bands between 5400 and 5600 feet that can be skied via gullies (have been skied on Nordic equipment). Less adventurous skiers can avoid the ravines by traversing to the west and following their tracks out to the road and back to the car.

MUIR SNOWFIELD

73

Map—
page 199

Start Point	Paradise Parking Lot, 5450 feet
High Point	Camp Muir, 10,000 feet
Best Time	October to June
Length	Day trip; 9 miles; 6 hours
Difficulty	Intermediate; navigation; moderate avalanche potential
Map	USGS 7.5-minute series, Mount Rainier East

The broad, low-angle southern slope of Mount Rainier rises from Paradise at 5440 feet to Camp Muir at 10,000 feet. The Muir Snowfield provides year-round skiing (in most years) from Camp Muir to Pebble Creek (about 7500 feet): Early-season tours (October and November) offer the best combination of snow conditions, weather, and entertainment value. Navigation skills are required for this tour since whiteouts occur frequently and the descent involves a broad, curving ridge with cliffs on either side.

Drive State Route 706 to the Nisqually entrance of Mount Rainier National Park. Continue to the Paradise parking lot adjacent to the ranger station. (No overnight camping is permitted in the parking lot.)

After inquiring at the ranger station about avalanche conditions, ascend the open slopes above the parking lot, keeping left of Alta Vista. In low-snow conditions, stay on designated trails to protect alpine vegetation. Ascend the broad, rolling ridge to the steep face of Panorama Point. If the trail is open, ascend it to the top of Panorama Point (6950 feet). Otherwise, ascend the slope on the windswept side.

This promontory frequently develops dangerous windslab conditions on the lee side. If there is significant avalanche danger around Panorama Point, you may avoid it entirely by skiing Paradise Glacier to Camp Muir (see Tour 75).

From Panorama Point, continue up the ridge in a northern direction. Cross Pebble Creek, pass McClure Rock (7390 feet) on the left (west) side, and continue to Anvil Rock (9580 feet). Pass this prominent point on the left — by now you can see the notch where Camp Muir is located — and ascend to the camp.

If clouds begin moving in, consider an immediate descent since skiing in whiteout conditions is unpleasant and dangerous. It is important to stay on the snowfield rather than descending right to the Nisqually Glacier (heavily crevassed this time of year) or descending too far left to the Paradise Glacier.

This is a serious tour. It requires warm clothing, sunscreen, and navigation skills. Clouds and wind can turn scorching heat to blizzard in minutes.

Returning from Camp Muir (Photo: Gary Brill).

NISQUALLY GLACIER

74

Start Point	Paradise Parking Lot, 5450 feet
High Point	Above Pebble Creek, 7600 feet
Best Time	February to April
Length	Day trip; 4 miles; 6 hours
Difficulty	Advanced; glacier skiing; high avalanche potential
Maps	USGS 7.5-minute series, Mount Rainier East and West

This tour is basically a one-way descent of a mighty glacier, the Nisqually. It is generally feasible only in midwinter, when heavy snowfall has covered the crevasses on the lower glacier. A good overview of the lower route is possible from Canyon Rim Viewpoint. The exit and pickup take place at the Nisqually River bridge just east of Nahunta Falls on the Paradise highway. Visibility must be good for this tour.

Descending the Nisqually Glacier near 7000 feet (Photo: Gary Brill).

Drive to Paradise and check with the ranger about avalanche and snowpack conditions. Climb over Panorama Point and McClure Rock to Sugarloaf, a promontory above Pebble Creek. Head west from Sugarloaf, looking for a couloir that descends to the Nisqually Moraine. Ski this 1500-foot slope (steep) but do not venture far out on the Nisqually. For a shorter tour, ascend only to Panorama Point and descend directly to the Nisqually.

Ski along the left (east) edge of the glacier until terrain forces you to the main glacier surface. Near the snout you may have to descend to the north side and hike out the last 0.5 mile if there is insufficient snow.

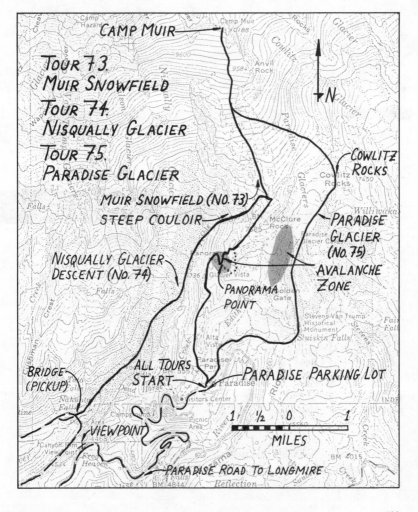

The west side of Paradise Glacier is an avoidable avalanche zone (Photo: Gary Brill).

PARADISE GLACIER

75

Map—
page 199

Start Point	Paradise Parking Lot, 5450 feet
High Point	Cowlitz Rocks or beyond, 7450 feet
Best Time	April to June
Length	Day trip; 7 miles; 6 hours
Difficulty	Intermediate; glacier travel; moderate avalanche potential; navigation
Map	USGS 7.5-minute series, Mount Rainier East

The Paradise Glacier lies just east of the Muir Snowfield and south of the massive Cowlitz Glacier. The Paradise Glacier is the site of the famous Paradise Ice Caves. The ice caves have been closed in recent years, but the glacier still offers excellent skiing. This tour affords a novel view of the south shoulder of Rainier and a chance to escape the hordes at Paradise and on the Muir snowfield. The terrain and exposure is well suited to spring touring. During high avalanche danger this is a good route to Camp Muir because it avoids the hazards of Panorama Point.

Drive to the Paradise parking lot. Behind the ranger station at Paradise is a trail heading right (northeast) to the Edith Creek basin. Cross Edith Creek and head northeast across the basin, past the rightmost stream. Climb the ridge on the right side of the stream to gain gentler terrain above. Head north for 1 mile, skiing up the narrow valley leading to the snout of Paradise Glacier. Avoid the left (west) cliffs since they frequently discharge rock and ice. The crux is a small rise near 6400 feet. If this appears stable, ascend it and continue close to Cowlitz Rocks, then climb to the upper Paradise Glacier. Descend by retracing the approach.

If you choose to go higher, you can cross the Paradise Glacier, an active, crevassed ice body, by heading northwest from the rise above Cowlitz Rocks. A broad, moderately steep ramp provides access to the Muir Snowfield between 8000 and 9000 feet.

Skiers have descended the Cowlitz Glacier from Camp Muir. This is a serious mountaineering descent due to avalanche potential, crevasses, and weather hazards.

WHITE PASS

76

Start Point	White Pass, 4470 feet
High Point	Hogback Mountain, 6790 feet
Best Time	December to April
Length	Day orip; 5 miles; 3 hours
Difficulty	Intermediate; moderate avalanche potential; navigation
Maps	Green Trails No. 303, White Pass; USGS 15-minute series, White Pass

Map— page 202

Hogback Mountain is a gentle summit adjacent to the White Pass ski area that offers miles of hills and grand views of Mount Rainier and Goat Rocks.

Drive U.S. 12 to the White Pass ski area. Park in the area lot and sign out at the ticket booth. Unless you seek an early start or are broke, ride the lift to the top of Pigtail Peak. It is definitely worth it to save your strength for the skiing ahead. From the top of the lift head straight ahead to the start of the Holiday Run, then descend 0.3 mile to a saddle. If indigent, contour around the left side of Pigtail to the same wooded saddle.

Head southwest along the broad saddle, following it through trees for 1 mile. Stay either on or near the left of the ridge top. After 1 mile the terrain opens up and skiing at many levels of difficulty becomes available. To continue to the summit of Hogback, pass a buttress on the right and continue to the ridge beyond, until you can go no more. You have arrived. Retrace your ascent route to return to the ski area.

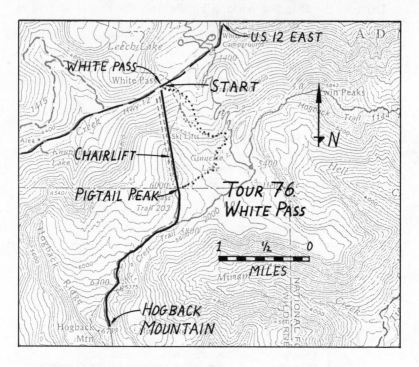

GOAT ROCKS

77

Start Point	Johnson Creek Road, 3000 feet
High Point	Old Snowy Mountain, 7930 feet
Best Time	November; April to June
Length	3 days; 16 miles; 14 hours
Difficulty	Advanced; navigation; moderate avalanche potential
Maps	Green Trails Nos. 302, 303, and 334, Packwood, White Pass, and Walupt Lake; USGS 15-minute series, Packwood, White Pass, and Walupt Lake

Goat Rocks are the glaciated massif visible to the southeast from the Muir Snowfield (see Tour 73). It is the southwestern slope of the

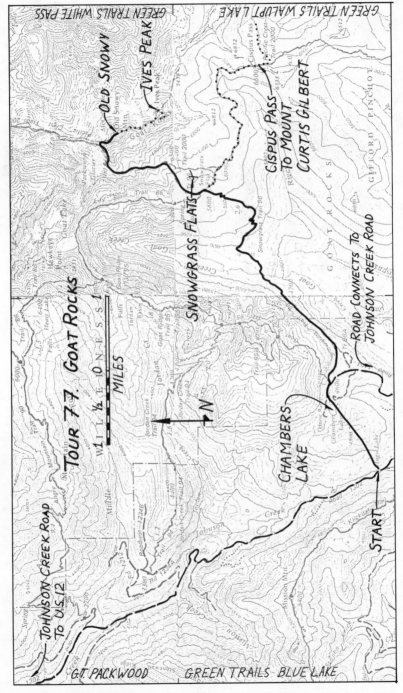

Approaching Goat Rocks, near Snow Grass Flats (Photo: Bryan Scott).

Goat Rocks that is most interesting to early-season backcountry skiers: Little snow is needed to enable tourers to take runs from 7900 to 6000 feet. Goat Rocks is a comfortable three-day trip with uncommon views of Mounts Adams, Rainier, and the truncated cone of St. Helens.

Drive U.S. 12 to Packwood. South of Packwood 2.5 miles turn east onto the Johnson Creek road and drive as far as road or snow conditions permit (you will have to drive out as well). Six miles from the U.S. 12 junction there is a switchback west of Jordan Creek. From here the road climbs 2 miles to meet the headwaters of Johnson Creek (a small lake). From the lake, ski east through the forest to Chambers Lake (about 0.7 mile).

On the north side of Chambers Lake is a vestigial road. Follow it (east) for 0.5 mile to the start of a trail. Follow the trail for 4 miles, heading northeast to Snowgrass Flats (6300 feet). Set up your tent in the shelter of trees northeast of the trail.

Skiing possibilities abound on the slopes above the flats. Nearby ski mountaineering objectives include Old Snowy (7930 feet) and Ives Peak (7900 feet). Mount Curtis Gilbert (8200 feet) requires half a day from Snowgrass Flats, skiing over Cispus Pass for both the ascent and the return. The east slopes of Goat Rocks also offer fine ski runs accessible from Snowgrass Flats (over the top and back again) or from McCall Basin. Reach McCall Basin from the north fork of the Tieton River.

This area is fairly exposed in terms of weather and distance from assistance. The backcountry skier is advised to ski conservatively and descend if there are signs of approaching bad weather.

MOUNT ADAMS

78

Start Point	Timberline Forest Camp, 6300 feet	
High Point	Mount Adams Summit, 12,310 feet	
Best Time	November; April to June	
Length	Overnight; 8 miles; 10 hours	
Difficulty	Advanced; low avalanche potential; navigation	
Maps	USGS 7.5-minute series, Mount Adams West and East; USGS 15-minute series, Mount Adams	

Map— page 206

The southern shoulder of Mount Adams enables skiers to ascend the entire mountain without setting foot on crevassed terrain. The

Mount Adams from the southwest; ski runs are possible down the ridge, and flanking gullies (Photo: U.S. Forest Service).

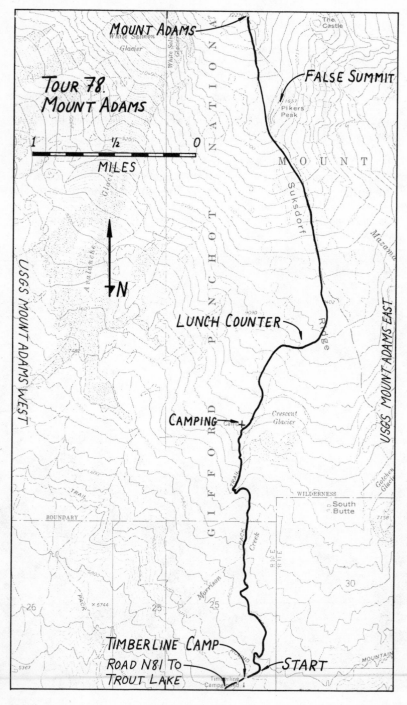

MOUNT ADAMS

FALSE SUMMIT

TOUR 78.
MOUNT ADAMS

1   ½   0

MILES

N

LUNCH COUNTER

USGS MOUNT ADAMS WEST

USGS MOUNT ADAMS EAST

CAMPING

TIMBERLINE CAMP
ROAD N81 TO
TROUT LAKE

START

long (4 miles) ridge offers the hardy skier a 6000-foot run! The only obstacle to complete enjoyment of the tour is exhaustion: After climbing to the summit, few skiers will be at the top of their form.

Leave State Route 14 (Columbia River Highway), and drive north on State Route 141. This highway follows the White Salmon River to the town of Trout Lake. Drive road No. N90 north for 3 miles to its junction with road No. N81. Drive N81 as far as conditions permit, all the way to Timberline Camp if possible (7.5 miles from the junction).

From Timberline Camp head north (12 degrees from true north) to the start of the south ridge, sometimes called Suksdorf Ridge. Follow this ridge due north to the Lunch Counter, a shoulder near 9000 feet.

At about 9700 feet, the slope steepens to the false summit (11,700 feet). The true summit lies just over the next hill, about 600 feet higher. It may be useful to wand the ascent route in case clouds obscure the descent.

If the ridge is windblown snow, better conditions for a ski descent may be found in the southwest chute, a shallow gully west of the south ridge, but east of the Avalanche Glacier. Be sure to evaluate avalanche potential before entering the gully. This route joins the snowfields to the left (west) of the south ridge; a traverse back to Timberline Camp completes the tour.

APPENDIX A:
TIPS FOR BACKCOUNTRY SKIERS

Equipment

Modern alpine touring equipment tends to be somewhat heavier than Nordic touring gear (about two pounds total for state-of-the-art equipment). The advantage of alpine touring equipment is increased security in difficult conditions such as ice, slush, or very steep terrain.

Boots. Alpine touring boots resemble alpine downhill boots except that they are lighter in weight, have plenty of forward flex, and have a lug sole for better off-ski traction. Lug soles require a plate

Skiing near Sherman Peak on Mount Baker — Tour 21 (Photo: Gary Brill).

binding to release effectively. A cross-country downhill boot (not a telemark racing boot) suffices for Nordic ski mountaineering.

Skis. Alpine touring skis are (ideally) lighter and shorter than alpine downhill skis and tend to have a general-purpose flex. Nordic mountaineering skis are wider than track-running skis, have metal edges, sidecut to assist the skier in carving turns, and little or no wax pocket (mostly you use skins for climbing). While modern skis rarely break, an extra pair of skis should be taken on trips into remote country.

A general recreational flex or combination ski is recommended for backcountry touring. Generally speaking, both tip and tail should be moderately flexible. Slalom or racing skis are inappropriate for backcountry touring because their specialized construction is unsuited to a wide range of snow conditions such as powder and ice. Many skiers prefer a ski that is about head height, plus or minus a few centimeters.

Climbing Aids. The most efficient means of ascending a snow slope is with the aid of climbing skins. Skins are long pieces of fabric with nylon bristles, mohair, or sealskin on one side, with the hair all pointing in the same direction. Most modern skins attach to the skis' running surface with a permanently tacky adhesive which lasts for many on-off cycles. Although the method of attachment may vary, the thing to look for is a system that keeps the edges of the ski exposed and the skin firmly attached, especially while on steep traverses. Positive fasteners at either end are very desirable. Silicone treatments can reduce the tendency of skins to become soaked in warmer weather. Very cold weather sometimes causes skin adhesive to lose its tack. In that case, warm the skins by wrapping them around your waist (or calves under your gaiters) for the descent. They'll regain their tack quickly.

If climbing skins do become soaked and won't stick to the skis, wax can save an afternoon. Much of the mystery of waxing skis for "kick" has been eliminated by the waxing guides provided free by the wax manufacturers. Properly applied, kicker wax allows the skier to ski undulating terrain without stopping to reapply skins.

If neither skins nor wax is available, lengths of cord or bootlaces wrapped around the skis can function like tire traction chains. This remedy is makeshift at best but does work. It is better to plan ahead and carry an extra set of lightweight skins in the party.

Harscheisen, small metal crampons that fit on the bottoms of alpine touring skis, are sometimes useful, especially in the morning on spring tours when the surface is frozen hard.

Bindings. Modern alpine touring bindings allow the skier to ski comfortably on flat or uphill terrain as well as downhill runs. This flexibility is achieved by hinging the binding at the toe and allowing the heel of the boot to rise slightly for skiing on flat or uphill terrain.

Crampons are useful for climbing crunchy morning snow (Photo: Gary Brill).

For an alpine-style descent, the skier locks the heels down and points the skis downhill. Most of these bindings aren't designed for lift skiing and don't offer all six release angles as conventional alpine bindings do. Alpine touring bindings are typically available only at mountaineering outlets — most stores professing to be ski stores do not, at this time, have either the merchandise or the expertise to advise the ski mountaineer properly.

Cross-country bindings for ski mountaineering are still restricted to the "Nordic Norm" (or 75 mm three-pin standard) or some cable version of it. The primary features to look for are a broad bail (the clamp that holds down the boot toe) that doesn't cut the boot leather, and a binding design that allows enough room for the sole thickness. Nordic skiers: Always carry an extra binding! To prevent the loss of a ski-binding bail, tie a light cord from the bail to the binding. They pop off in unlikely places!

Alpine touring bindings accept boots ranging from plastic mountaineering boots to alpine ski touring boots (not to mention downhill ski boots). While the versatility of wearing one pair of mountaineering boots for both skiing and climbing is attractive, the ankle flexibility required in mountain boots lowers the degree of control and safety available to you while skiing. Equally important, mountain boots lessen the effectiveness of the binding-release system. If you wear alpine touring boots with lug soles, make sure you are using a plate-type binding. Current non-plate bindings may not release properly when used with lug-soled boots.

Poles. Strong alpine-style poles are adequate for ski touring. Pick ones with larger, sturdy baskets and be sure to carry extra baskets. Not only should the baskets be large, they should also be firm for trudging through deep snow. Track skiing or Nordic racing poles tend to be too light and weak and too long. Weak poles break and long poles induce high-handed skiing, which is unstable, tiring, and unsightly. Be sure to remove your hands from the wrist loops while skiing through trees or brush. Catching a basket could result in a dislocated shoulder.

Long poles, however, are better if a lot of flat travel is expected, or you are skiing very deep powder.

Special touring poles with self-arrest grips and the ability to convert into avalanche probes are available. While the efficacy of the self-arrest grips is controversial, the need for avalanche probes has been well-established: Probe poles should be considered standard equipment on backcountry tours.

Backcountry skiers must become proficient at using their poles for self-arrest in case of a slip on steep slopes. When you fall, let go of one ski pole and grasp the other one by its grip and by the shaft just above the basket. Vigorously use the point of the pole to stop sliding down the slope. See Vic Bein's *Mountain Skiing* for an excellent discussion of this technique. Do not ski downhill with an ice ax in your hand because of the danger of self-impalement.

Ski Restraints. The issue of ski restraint must be addressed by every skier. In lift-served areas, skiers are required to use brakes or runaway straps. Runaway straps are essential in the backcountry where a runaway ski could fall into a crevasse or off a cliff. A real problem arises, however, when you are skiing in avalanche terrain. No one ever expects to get caught, but if you are, having runaway straps on may increase the likelihood of your being injured by your skis. One possible solution is "powder cords," five- to eight-foot cords attached to the skis, tied to you, and tucked inside your gaiters. If you crash, the skis are retained. If you get caught in an avalanche, the cords permit some distance between you and your skis.

Kneepads. Kneepads should be seriously considered by inveterate telemarkers, especially in low-snow conditions since the trailing knee is exposed to potentially serious injury from contact with concealed rocks, stumps, and other terrain features. Kneepads help reduce the frequency of this kind of needlessly disabling injury. Basketball-style kneepads are adequate and can be worn inside trousers.

Clothing

While clothing is a personal matter, general principles do apply. Cotton has no place in the ski mountaineer's wardrobe because of its drastically reduced insulating power when wet. Layered clothing, starting with polypropylene or some other nonabsorbent layer, provides effective temperature control. Enough clothing should be taken so that the skier could spend the night out (albeit uncomfortably) if necessary.

Some skiers wear two pairs of thick wool socks, while others wear a thin "sliding layer" and a thick pair to prevent blisters. Still others report satisfactory results with synthetics such as polypropylene. Feet should not feel constricted—the resulting loss of circulation will guarantee cold feet. Vapor-barrier socks are claimed to keep feet warmer longer. Antiperspirant (not deodorant) on your feet elimi-

A fashionably dressed skier on the Carbon Glacier — Tour 68 (Photo: Gary Brill).

nates sweating for 12 to 16 hours, resulting in warmer feet in cold weather. It should be applied daily for the duration of the tour.

High gaiters are essential for keeping snow out of socks and boots. While this is less important on late spring or summer day trips, it becomes vital in winter or on overnight trips because of the misery caused by cold, wet feet. For extremely cold weather, insulated "super gaiters," covering the entire boot, help keep your feet toasty. Warm-up pants or bib overalls that zip up the sides allow the skier to put on or take off trousers without removing skis or boots, often a welcome procedure.

Light wool, or synthetic pile shirts or sweaters topped off with a wind shell (when needed) generally provide as much warmth as a person needs while actually skiing. A skier may bring more clothing to put on at rest stops and at lunch breaks.

For protection against precipitation, an anorak or "Cascade parka" and rainpants provide temporary shelter. "Breathable" fabrics provide adequate wind- and weather-proofing under normal skiing conditions. A light silk or polypropylene balaclava and a heavier wool or pile hat, with ear and neck protection, suffice for the head. Light gloves, heavier mittens of wool or pile, and mitten shells will protect the skier's hands in most conditions found in the Cascades.

Many of the ski tours described in this book are excellent spring or summer trips. Summer temperatures are often quite temperate, and skiers frequently make their gloveless ascents in shorts and T-shirts. In this case, protection against abrasions from falls and wind or sunburn is essential. But alpine conditions can change rapidly from sweltering heat to a cold, driving rain. The key to effective use of your clothing is keeping your body in a state of equilibrium: Keep it fed and watered, dry, and at a comfortable temperature.

Impedimenta

Backcountry travelers are on their own. While the feeling of independence in untracked terrain is one of the special treats of ski mountaineering, this independence requires that skiers carry with them the capability to feed, shelter, and warm themselves and, under certain circumstances, to effect self-rescue.

A pack suitable for ski touring should be soft (or internal frame) and roomy, equipped with a waist strap and with ski-carrying patches on its sides. A rucksack that is too small becomes a chore to repack after a lunch or clothing break. A minor, but convenient, feature is the proper location of the top-flap zipper: It should face toward the shoulder strap, so that when the skier removes the pack to reach into the top flap, he can lay the pack on the snow without getting snow or dirt all over the surface that will soon be touching his back again.

The following standard mountain travel items should be inside the pack:

1 Extra clothing, wrapped in plastic to keep it dry.
2 Extra food, enough for an emergency meal.
3 Extra sunglasses or goggles.
4 Knife.
5 Matches in waterproof container. Butane lighters are wonderful... until a drop of rain or a snowflake dampens the striker wheel. Why not carry both matches and lighter?
6 Chemical firestarter for wet wood. Above timberline a stove and small pot are essential.
7 First-aid kit, with a heavy emphasis on treating bleeding-type injuries from ski-edge cuts. *Medicine for Mountaineering* is a good reference source.
8 Flashlight with spare batteries and bulb. A headlamp may be handier.
9 Topographic maps. (This guidebook doesn't count.)
10 Compass. An altimeter is a useful luxury, both for navigation and weather observations on longer trips.
11 Wide-mouth water bottle and water.
12 An appetizing lunch, including lots of high-energy types of food. The mountains are no place to conduct a weight-loss program.
13 Sunscreen, including lip coating. Minimum SPF 15.
14 Two large plastic garbage sacks for emergency bivouacs.
15 Personal hygiene articles.

Besides standard mountain travel equipment, the following equipment should be carried on backcountry ski trips:

1 Avalanche transceiver (one per person). Batteries should be fresh and all units must be compatible. Practice finding a buried transceiver during sunny lunch breaks. Practice!
2 Unbreakable snow shovel. (A two-year warranty does little good if your buried partner has to wait until the manufacturer sends you a replacement.) One per person.
3 Avalanche probe poles. At least one set per pair of skiers.
4 Ski wax and scraper; an assortment suitable for likely conditions; also, wax remover for late-season trips to remove pollen from running surfaces.
5 Repair kit: including picture-hanging wire, spare screws and bolts for bindings, extra bindings, extra ski-pole basket, screwdrivers, pliers or vise-grip, duct tape, five-minute epoxy, heavy string or cord, heavy-duty sewing needle and thread. This kit should be carried with you whenever you are on skis. On a tour in Canada's Coast Range, one of our party suffered an acute binding failure near the top of a 2000-foot

Roped glacier skiing (Photo: Gary Brill).

run through knee-deep powder. Not only did the fellow miss
out on the run, he also had to ski four miles back to camp on
one ski!

6   A spare set of lightweight skins. One per party.

Some of the trips in this guide involve ascents of glaciers or short
sections of steep terrain. Useful equipment includes the following:

1   Ice ax.
2   Crampons, sometimes. Take crampons whenever a tour has a
    mandatory steep section. You can never tell when something
    will be icy. Make certain that they have been adjusted before
    you leave on the tour.
3   Nine-mm rope (40 to 50 meters for two to three persons),
    snow pickets, one or two ice screws, prusik slings, carabiners
    and pulleys, and wands (for marking crevasses).

Practice and discuss the use of these items with your party prior to
setting out on a "bold" tour. Taking part in an alpine travel course is
strongly recommended.

Touring Techniques

Learning to ski unpacked snow. Skiing the unpacked edges of
intermediate runs in ski areas is an efficient way for novice Nordic
and alpine skiers to get enough practice at turning in the type of

Sometimes it's more efficient to climb without skis (Photo: Gary Brill).

snow encountered in the backcountry. Short forays into the woods adjacent to ski areas are a good way to start the process of becoming a backcountry skier. Skiers should never ski closed runs, however.

Routefinding. When skiing, choose a route that contours around obstacles rather than goes directly over them. Such a route requires the least energy output and will generally minimize avalanche hazard (with exceptions). Avoid very steep hills with skins on your skis since it is difficult to edge effectively. The trick is to use enough edge to keep from sliding sideways while keeping enough of the climbing skin on the snow to keep from sliding backward. Generally you are better off picking a route that minimizes the overall slope angle. Side-stepping and herringboning are slow and inefficient. Avoid using these techniques in the backcountry.

If some in the party have skins and others are using waxless skis or wax for traction, have someone with skins break trail. The trail breaker should make certain that the track is gentle enough for "waxers" to follow. Uphill kick turns can reduce steep-hill anxiety. In the event you find yourself in an extremely steep traverse, you can increase your feeling of security by putting both poles together and bracing yourself on the uphill side, then stepping carefully to safety. If you slip, you can use the two poles together for self-arrest (like an ice ax).

Avoid this risky situation by looking and planning ahead. Some slopes are so steep that it becomes more efficient simply to remove skis and climb on foot. Hold one ski in each hand and ram the tails of the skis into the snow with each step while allowing the poles to dangle from the wrists. Attempting to remove skis in the middle of a steep hill is an invitation to disaster.

Skiing Techniques. The primary element in backcountry skiing is the carved turn. While groomed slopes permit both Nordic and alpine skiers to skid telemarks and parallel turns, the variable snow in the backcountry (similar to the unpacked, tracked crud adjacent to ski runs) would throw a skier attempting to skid turns. Try to carve all your turns.

The reduced fore-and-aft stability of Nordic equipment may be compensated for (when necessary) by assuming the telemark stance, even while parallel skiing. Place one ski ahead of the other (either ski) and make parallel turns, wedelns, or lateral projections (side-stepped turns) as desired.

Cranking a high-speed telemark below Coleman Pinnacle — Tour 5 (Photo: Gary Brill).

Alpine and Nordic skiers travel through deep powder using similar techniques. All turns are carved, and unweighting is done using leg retraction (up-unweighting) with emphasis on even-weighting and smooth transitions between turns. On skinny skis, assume the telemark position if obstacles or terrain features are encountered.

Windblown, breakable crust can be skied using a combination of techniques and one basic principle: Jump telemark, jump parallel, or make all your movements very precise. The final option, of course, is to walk or glissade down.

Jump telemarks are just that: a strong edge set with pole plant, followed by a spring into the air and a midair lead change or stepover. The skier literally jumps from telemark stance to telemark stance.

Alpine skiers can blast through crust by using jump or "windshield wiper" turns. Both edges are set and weighted equally at the conclusion of this turn. On very steep slopes, it sometimes helps to plant both poles simultaneously. This is decidedly a turn for the hardy. Vic Bein's *Mountain Skiing* and Ned Gillette's *Cross-Country Skiing* offer detailed and understandable descriptions of advanced telemark and parallel techniques. Steve Barnett's *Cross-Country Downhill,* Third Edition, is especially instructive about skiing difficult Northwest snow.

"Impossible snow" can sometimes be avoided by careful selection of the descent route: The lee side of a windswept ridge often has pockets of powder in midwinter (but be careful of windslab conditions). Sometimes the snow on forested slopes stays soft much longer than on open, windswept slopes (see Mount Margaret, Tour 53). Sun-warmed slopes offer pleasant corn snow, but the same run can turn icy minutes after the sun sets (see Mount Baker, Easton Glacier Tour 22). If conditions are truly unskiable, it may be safer to simply doff the skis and hike out: Falling at the conclusion of every turn does little for your spirits, technique, or physical well-being.

Staying Well in the Backcountry

The first rule of safety is to be observant. Be aware of your own body and equipment, of your party, of the weather, and of the mountain terrain and its snow cover. Observe actively.

Stay dry. Staying dry is essential for keeping warm in winter woods. Wet clothing is always uncomfortable, sometimes life-threatening. Do not assume that "It's all right to get wet since we're skiing out shortly." You may unexpectedly be forced to bivouac and find yourself in a real emergency.

Don't overheat. An important part of cold-weather adaptation is preventing yourself from overheating. Remove hats, shell garments,

Lenticular clouds sometimes augur bad weather (Photo: Rainer Burgdorfer).

and sweaters, and possibly gaiters, as you begin to warm up during the first part of the tour to minimize perspiration. Simultaneously, slow the pace to keep cool. Be sure, however, that removing hats or ear protection does not expose nose, cheeks, or ears to frostbite.

Avoid cold injuries. When snow or rain begins to fall, put on shell garments to keep fuzzy sweaters, mittens, and hats dry. Move more slowly to reduce heat output and perspiration.

Avoid becoming chilled. Chilled and exhausted, you are well on your way to hypothermia, a potentially fatal lowering of the body's core temperature. Carrying a light stove to "brew up" can increase your comfort level and safety margin significantly.

Symptoms of hypothermia include uncontrollable shivering, disorientation, and loss of appetite. Hypothermia must be treated as a life-threatening emergency. Warm liquids and dry clothing must be administered to the victim immediately.

Very cold weather brings with it mixed blessings. Snow conditions tend to be better and insulation tends to stay drier, but the danger of frostnip and frostbite increases drastically. Frostnip is a superficial cold injury to extremities, which is easily treated by simply warming the afflicted area. Frostbite is a serious injury in which the afflicted body part is actually frozen, with resulting cellular damage. Immediate evacuation and medical care by those experienced in frostbite treatment are called for in case of frostbite. Under no circumstances should the frozen body part be thawed or rubbed while in the field. Again, immediate evacuation and treatment by medical persons experienced in frostbite treatment are required.

These injuries are easily prevented by making certain boots and mittens are warm and don't fit too snugly, that faces are covered during very cold or windy conditions, and that mittens are well mended and secured. For warmth, wear mittens instead of gloves. Some skiers secure their mittens with cords to prevent loss. Having the wind whisk your mittens away becomes serious if you have no extras!

An important part of frost injury (and hypothermia) prevention is proper nourishment. Eat! Drink! It is very easy to get dehydrated in very cold weather. Dehydration leads to chemical imbalance, making production of body heat less efficient, which leads to frostnip, and so on.

Are your feet very cold and getting colder? Put on more clothing and have a snack. Slip an extra set of wool socks *over* your boots. The snow sticks to the fuzzy sock but the arrangement keeps your toes toasty. Super gaiters can help keep your feet warm on those icy January days. If you find that you are not properly equipped for the tour, borrow clothing from your companions, descend to a lower elevation, or cancel the tour immediately. Playing the silent sufferer or trying to tough it out only jeopardizes your health and the pleasure of the tour.

When it becomes evident that you must spend an unexpected night out, decide on a suitable bivouac site allowing plenty of time to make yourself comfortable before nightfall if possible. Look for a site that is out of the wind, such as inside a thicket of alpine dwarf firs.

Avoid heat injuries. Spring and summer bring longer days, corn snow, and sunny weather: a perfect combination for excellent tours and... heat and radiation injuries. (Experienced skiers realize that sunburn is a hazard in winter as well as in summer.) Shield yourself with clothing, quality mountaineering sun glasses or goggles, and sun-screening agents with an SPF greater than 15. The creative use of on-hand materials can sometimes protect the skier from unanticipated sunshine.

Preventive measures for heat injuries include drinking plenty of water or electrolyte-replacement drinks, eating a balanced diet, wearing proper clothing, and maintaining a comfortable rate of travel. Drink plenty of water before your throat is parched. By that time it's too late — you're already dehydrated.

Prevent Giardiasis. Giardia must be presumed endemic to the Cascades. Bring all your water with you or boil or treat the water chemically. Two quarts of water per person on warm days or on strenuous tours is not too much. Replenishing your water bottle from freshly fallen snow is a way to keep from running out of water while on the move.

Bivouac in an emergency. When it becomes evident that you must spend an unexpected night out, decide on a suitable bivouac site immediately, before nightfall if possible. Take inventory of your equipment and your immediate surroundings. Is there plenty of accessible firewood? Is it feasible to dig a snow cave? Do you have a functioning stove with fuel? Do you have a sleeping bag? Answers to these questions will determine how you should best prepare for the night. If there is plenty of firewood, you could build and tend a warm fire all night; you'll be warm even if you don't get any sleep. If wood is not available, look for a site that is out of the wind, perhaps inside a thicket of alpine dwarf firs. Windproof the shelter with snow blocks, or dig a snow cave (see *Mountaineering: The Freedom of the Hills,* 4th edition). Do not get wet or exhausted while digging your shelter. Try to locate or melt enough drinking water to get through the night. Don't eat snow; melt it first. Put on all your clothes, loosen your ski boots or remove them entirely, and huddle together for warmth. Put your feet in your rucksack. Contact lens wearers, remove your lenses and keep them from freezing. Eat frequently to keep up your energy throughout the night. Don't be afraid: Plenty of others have spent nights out in the open and survived in fine shape. Keep your spirits up!

Move out at first light, being extra careful not to get hurt or lost; with lowered reserves you are even more susceptible to injury.

Effective sun protection can be obtained by creative use of on-hand materials (Photo: Rainer Burgdorfer).

Trees on Mazama Ridge receive the brunt of Pacific storms (Photo: Gary Brill).

APPENDIX B:
RECOMMENDED READING

Avalanches

Daffern, Tony. *Avalanche Safety for Skiers and Climbers*. Calgary: Rocky Mountain Books, 1983.

LaChapelle, Edward R. *The ABC of Avalanche Safety*, 2nd ed. Seattle: The Mountaineers, 1985.

Perla, Ronald I. *Modern Avalanche Rescue*, USDA.

Perla, Ronald I., and Martinelli, M. *Avalanche Handbook A89*, USDA, revised 1978.

Routes

Beckey, Fred. *Cascade Alpine Guide*, vol. 1-3. Seattle: The Mountaineers, 1986, 1977, 1981.

Kirkendall, Tom, and Spring, Vicky. *Cross-Country Ski Trails of Washington's Cascades and Olympics*. Seattle: The Mountaineers, 1983.

Mueller, Ted. *Northwest Ski Trails*. Seattle: The Mountaineers, 1968 (out of print).

Portman, Sally. *Ski Touring Methow Style*. Lynnwood: Washington Trails Association, 1986.

Spring, Ira, and Manning, Harvey. *50 Hikes in Mount Rainier National Park*, 2nd ed. Seattle: The Mountaineers, 1978.

———. *100 Hikes in the North Cascades*, 3rd ed. Seattle: The Mountaineers, 1986.

Skiing and Ski Mountaineering

Barnett, Steve. *Cross-Country Downhill and Other Nordic Mountain Skiing Techniques*, 3rd ed. Seattle: Pacific Search Press, 1983.

Bein, Vic. *Mountain Skiing*. Seattle: The Mountaineers, 1982.

Peters, Ed. *Mountaineering: The Freedom of the Hills*, 4th ed. Seattle: The Mountaineers, 1982.

First Aid

Lathrop, Theodore. *Hypothermia: Killer of the Unprepared*. Portland: Mazamas, 1972.

Wilkerson, James A. *Medicine for Mountaineering*, 3rd ed. Seattle: The Mountaineers, 1985.

———, Ed. *Hypothermia, Frostbite and Other Cold Injuries: Prevention, Recognition, Pre-Hospital Treatment*. Seattle: The Mountaineers, 1986.

APPENDIX C:
SEASONAL CROSS REFERENCE

Use these tables to pick tours suitable for a given month. For example, if it is October, where are some places that are likely to offer good skiing? First decide on a general region; for example, the Mount Baker area. Next, look in the top row for the current month, then trace down the appropriate column. The bullet indicates a tour that may be suitable for the given month, depending on weather conditions.

Mount Baker Highway

Tour	Jan	Feb	Mar	Apr	May	Jun	Jul	Aug	Sep	Oct	Nov	Dec
1. Chowder Ridge							•	•	•	•		
2. Ruth Mountain				•	•	•	•					
3. Shuksan Arm	•	•	•	•							•	•
4. Lake Ann Butte	•	•	•	•								•
5. Coleman Pinnacle	•	•	•	•	•	•				•	•	•
6. Sholes Glacier				•	•	•	•	•	•	•		
7. Mount Herman	•	•	•								•	•
8. Coleman Glacier				•	•	•				•	•	

North Cascades Highway

Tour	Jan	Feb	Mar	Apr	May	Jun	Jul	Aug	Sep	Oct	Nov	Dec
9. Silver Star Mountain				•	•							
10. Early Winters Spires				•	•	•						
11. Black Peak				•	•	•	•					

Month

Tour	Jan	Feb	Mar	Apr	May	Jun	Jul	Aug	Sep	Oct	Nov	Dec
12. Snowfield Peak		●	●	●	●	●						
13. Teebone Ridge	●		●	●	●	●						●
14. Eldorado				●	●	●						
15. Boston Basin				●	●	●						
16. Sahale Arm			●	●	●	●						
17. Snowking Mountain				●	●	●						
18. Anderson Butte					●	●						
19. Bacon Peak					●	●	●					
20. Mount Shuksan		●	●	●	●	●						
21. Mount Baker/ Boulder Glacier					●	●	●					
22. Mount Baker/ Easton Glacier				●	●	●	●	●				
23. Morovitz Meadows				●	●	●						
24. Twin Sisters				●	●	●						

Mountain Loop Highway

Month

Tour	Jan	Feb	Mar	Apr	May	Jun	Jul	Aug	Sep	Oct	Nov	Dec
25. Glacier Peak					●	●						
26. Honeycomb/ Suiattle					●	●	●					
27. Meadow Mountain				●	●						●	
28. Green/ Buckindy				●	●	●					●	

Tour	Jan	Feb	Mar	Apr	May	Jun	Jul	Aug	Sep	Oct	Nov	Dec
29. Dome Glacier				●	●	●	●					
30. Whitehorse Mountain		●	●	●	●							
31. Mount Pilchuck	●	●	●									●

Stevens Pass Highway

Tour	Jan	Feb	Mar	Apr	May	Jun	Jul	Aug	Sep	Oct	Nov	Dec
32. Mount Hinman					●	●						
33. Cowboy Mountain	●	●	●	●								●
34. Heather Ridge	●	●	●									●
35. Yodelin	●	●	●									
36. Jove Peak	●	●	●									●
37. Jim Hill Mountain	●	●	●	●								
38. Rock Mountain				●	●					●	●	
39. Mount Howard	●	●	●									●
40. Nason Ridge	●	●	●	●								●
41. Chiwaukum Mountains				●	●							
42. Mount Maude				●	●	●						
43. Chiwawa Mountain				●	●	●						
44. Clark Mountain			●	●	●							

Month

Tour	Jan	Feb	Mar	Apr	May	Jun	Jul	Aug	Sep	Oct	Nov	Dec
45. Icicle Ridge	●	●										●
46. Dragontail Peak				●	●							
47. Porcupine Creek			●	●	●							
48. Ingalls Peak				●	●							
49. Mount Stuart				●	●							

Snoqualmie Pass

Month

Tour	Jan	Feb	Mar	Apr	May	Jun	Jul	Aug	Sep	Oct	Nov	Dec
50. Mount Daniel			●	●	●	●						
51. Jolly Mountain			●	●	●	●						
52. Amabilis Mountain	●	●	●									●
53. Mount Margaret	●	●	●									●
54. Kendall Ridge	●	●	●									
55. Red Mountain	●	●	●	●								
56. Mount Snoqualmie	●	●	●									●
57. Chair Peak	●	●	●	●								
58. Silver Peak	●	●	●	●								
59. Humpback Mountain		●	●	●								
60. Granite Mountain		●	●									

Mount Rainier and Areas South

Tour	Jan	Feb	Mar	Apr	May	Jun	Jul	Aug	Sep	Oct	Nov	Dec
61. Norse Peak	●	●	●	●								
62. Silver Basin	●	●	●	●							●	●
63. Chinook Pass											●	
64. Chinook to Crystal				●							●	
65. Summerland			●	●	●	●				●	●	
66. Interglacier					●	●						
67. Sunrise					●	●					●	
68. Carbon Glacier				●	●	●						
69. Russell Glacier						●	●			●	●	
70. Puyallup Cleaver					●	●	●					
71. Van Trump Park	●	●	●	●								
72. Tatoosh Range	●	●	●	●	●							●
73. Muir Snowfield	●	●	●	●	●	●				●	●	●
74. Nisqually Glacier	●	●	●	●								
75. Paradise Glacier					●	●	●					
76. White Pass	●	●	●	●								●
77. Goat Rocks				●	●	●					●	
78. Mount Adams				●	●	●					●	

INDEX

RAINER BURGDORFER, a Seattle resident, has been exploring the ridges, slopes, faces and valleys of the Cascades on skis and foot for 23 years. He prepared this guide to lure fellow skiers away from the known and the ordinary, to the less explored and more challenging terrain of the backcountry. Says Burgdorfer, "I was attracted to backcountry skiing by the tremendous freedoms it offers: freedom from lift lines, freedom to cover greater distances than possible on foot, and freedom to find the best possible skiing."

Burgdorfer first started skiing in 1961, adding mountaineering in 1973 following a climbing course at the University of Washington. He has climbed extensively in Washington and Yosemite, Calif., including guiding climbs on Mt. Rainier and participating in mountain rescues.